*The Wisdom of the East*

EDITED BY J. L. CRANMER-BYNG M.C.

# THE LIFE OF MILAREPA

# THE LIFE OF
# MILAREPA

*Tibet's Great Yogi*

## LOBZANG JIVAKA

**Condensed and adapted**
**from the original translation of**
**W. Y. Evans-Wentz**

Facsimile reprint 1994,
by LLANERCH PUBLISHERS,
Felinfach.

ISBN 1 897853 63 7.

*The original translation by W. Y. Evans-Wentz
was published by Oxford University Press
in 1928*

*To His Holiness the Dalai Lama*
*and his brother monks*
*in exile*

The object of the Editor of this series is a very
definite one. He desires above all things that
these books shall be the ambassadors of good-
will between East and West. He hopes that
they will contribute to a fuller knowledge of
the great cultural heritage of the East, for only
through real understanding will the West be
able to appreciate the underlying problems and
aspirations of Asia to-day. He is confident
that a deeper knowledge of the great ideals
and lofty philosophy of Eastern thought will
help to a revival of that true spirit of charity
which neither despises nor fears the nations
of another creed and colour.

J. L. CRANMER-BYNG

50 ALBEMARLE STREET

LONDON, W.1

# Contents

# Foreword

1066 is a date familiar to every Western schoolboy; to every Tibetan a date equally well known is 1052, for in that year there was born in a place called Kyanga-Tsa a boy who was destined to become in his lifetime one of the world's greatest *Yogis*—although to-day even less than half the world has as yet heard of him. Shortly after his death in 1135, his biography was written down by one of his chief disciples, Rechung. The biography is still extant. There is an excellent version in French by M. Bacot and it has also been translated into English and edited by W. Y. Evans-Wentz, in conjunction with his late *Guru*, Lama Kazi Dawa Samdup; it is from their book, with Dr Evans-Wentz's permission, that this story has been drawn.

It is the mark of a great work to be timeless; no date or era can be ascribed to it, so that it appeals equally to contemporaries and to descendants. It is this factor of timelessness that has made Shakespeare the greatest playwright the world has ever seen and this factor, too, is present in the biography of Jetsun Milarepa, whose trials and tribulations, as he sought for Enlightenment and Teaching, can find an echo in the hearts of many persons to-day whose aims are less ambitious. Milarepa was first and foremost a human being, but a human being who triumphed so successfully over all obstacles through singleness of purpose that by the time of his death he had become a superman. His story is an inspiration to all those who feel that circumstances weigh against them and that their ends are unattainable.

## Foreword

Since inspiration such as this is urgently required in the world to-day, and since the story makes such attractive and easy reading, a popular edition of Dr Evans-Wentz's more learned work may perhaps not be out of place. An attempt, therefore, has been made to reproduce the biography omitting the songs, some of the teaching, the more difficult designations, the more obscure references and the oriental discursiveness. I have brought the conversation into line with modern diction, so that the name of Milarepa may become as much a household word outside Tibet as it is within that great country, and so that some of the lessons to be drawn from his life may not be lost to the present generation.

The hero of the story, Jetsun Milarepa, is a lovable person whose ups and downs and his reactions to them, will evoke a response in the reader. His wicked Uncle and Aunt, too, will be familiar to all, for they have their counterpart in many a fairy tale, but their fate differs from that of the others, since retribution does not overtake them permanently and the Buddhist Doctrine that 'Hate is not conquered by Hate but by Love' is exemplified. The wife of Marpa, Milarepa's *Guru*, is portrayed as a typical housewife, kindly and sympathetic towards her protégé, as she tries to shield him from his Master's angry and often violent outbursts, comforts him with dainties to eat, dresses his sores and encourages him to persevere, finally conspiring with him to deceive her husband and to win for Milarepa the Teaching he has striven for so hard and long.

The minor characters are equally skilfully drawn. There are the curious sightseers who come to gaze upon the naked and emaciated hermit; the hunters who ransack his cave for forage, and who, when he will not admit to having any food, pick him up and drop him several times, a mere bag of bones to sport with; his sister who does not share his aims and would

x

*Foreword*

rather see him a fashionable and popular Lama, supported by
devoted disciples and lacking nothing of worldly things; his
mother who greets him with a broomstick handle when he
arrives home over-cheerful after imbibing the local beer too
freely at a party; all these and many others help to create a
story, the setting of which could as well be in India or modern
Europe to-day as in ancient Tibet.

Milarepa was not only a great Yogi, he was also a poet and
singer, it being recorded that he had a very fine voice; some
of his compositions, as contained in the original text and translation, have been paraphrased here. If the mind is too sophisti-
cated to accept the details of the biography as true, at all events
let it be remembered that Milarepa is a historical figure, a man
who has lived and died; and that the occult powers developed
in him have, after all, been known to the East as facts for
centuries past, whatever the West may have to say about
them. They come incidentally with mental development and
self-discipline, and should never be sought for their own sake,
as then the motive for their acquisition is wrong. These
powers came to Milarepa as his evolution unfolded.

Let those who read, therefore, do so prepared to find and
enjoy a human story and let those who are too superior to
believe it true, turn back to their space-ships, atom-splitting
and making of artificial rain!

# Introduction

This is an explanation of certain points that may arise in the mind of the non-Buddhist reader and may be read either before or after the main story.

## THE NAME MILAREPA

In recent years it has become fashionable to extend the transliteration of Tibetan words into English to names, with the result that they become unrecognisable and wrongly pronounced. The Tibetan alphabet does not lend itself to transliteration since the addition of one letter-sign to another letter does not result in the sounding of the two letters but of a third utterly different letter. Thus *p* + *y* is *ch* and not *pya* as one would expect. This has now happened to the name of Milarepa, transliterated into *Mi-la-ras-pa*, and therefore tending to make it pronounced Milaraspa. But the addition of *s* to a consonant without a vowel sign is to change what would normally be a short *a* (*ră* in this case) into *è* (like the French *è*), hence the correct pronunciation of Milarepa as it was originally written. The phonetic system would, therefore, seem the most useful one to use for Tibetan words as at least they are then comprehensible when spoken to a Tibetan. He can make nothing of transliteration, even if he can read a little English.

## A BASIC FALLACY

It is necessary right from the beginning to clear up a fallacy

## The Life of Milarepa

that is repeated over and over again by writers on Tibet. Its religion they please to term 'Lamaism', a name given originally by the British and other Western writers and travellers who have recorded their experiences in that mysterious land beyond the Himalayas, so difficult of entry and so well-stocked in Knowledge that has long been lost to the rest of the world.

*Lama* is a word used universally *outside* Tibet to indicate a Tibetan monk. Within Tibet it is used in its correct sense of *Guru* or Teacher. Some Tibetan monks are Lamas, many are not. Some Tibetan laymen are Lamas. From this initial error, which any Tibetan will readily correct, has arisen a second fallacy that some sects of Tibetan Buddhism permit their monks to marry, due to the fact that there are married Lamas in evidence.

To make this point quite clear and to give the analogous terminology for different classes of persons connected with Religious Teaching, I give the following table showing the corresponding English, Sanskrit, Pali and Tibetan terms.

| English | Pali | Sanskrit | Tibetan |
|---|---|---|---|
| Monk | Bhikkhu | Bhikshu | Gelong |
| Novice-monk | Samanera | Sramanera | Getsul |
| Teacher | Garu | Guru | Lama |
| Disciple | Chela (Hindi) | Shishya | Lobma |
| Real Incarnation | (Bodhisatta) | (Bodhisattva) | Tulku (Rimpoche) |

The commonly met-with, so-called Lama, attired in dark red skirt and cloak and with brocaded, sleeveless waistcoat, is, then, not necessarily a Lama, but he is a *gelong*. He may or may not be a Lama as well, if he is recognised as a Teacher and has

2

disciples or pupils. Hence what is derogatorily called Lamaism is the Tibetan form of Buddhism, incorporating Tantrayana (see below), Mahayana and Hinayana.

The *getsul* wears the same robes as the gelong but with a
simpler patterned skirt.

The *shishya* or *chela* (pronounced 'chayla')—I have used
the latter term in this book as it is more familiar to those
readers who will remember it from Kipling's great classic,
*Kim*—may be lay or ordained. If ordained he may be getsul
or gelong, for he always remains a chela in respect of those
who have been his Gurus or Lamas. Indeed, even a High
Lama, that is an advanced Initiate, may still be in chela–Guru
relationship, as in this story Ngogdun-Chudor was throughout his life to his master Marpa; Marpa himself would make
obeisance to his own Guru Naropa whenever he met him,
despite the lofty dignity to which he had himself attained.

## GURU–CHELA RELATIONSHIP

This brings us to the second point, and it is one that would
hardly have to be mentioned to an Eastern reader but which
is a pitfall to many a Westerner going East in search of a
Teacher and Teaching. The Guru–chela relationship is well
recognised and accepted in the East. It is unknown in this
form in the West, and more is the pity, for the observance of
it is the only means by which Higher Learning can be trans-
mitted.

The average Westerner blunders his way into the presence
of a Guru or Lama of whom he may have heard and behaves
according to his own country's ideas of courtesy and no more.
He demands this and that and he may even dictate to the
Teacher what and how he is to be taught and the length of

time at the Teacher's disposal for this instruction, which is the
length of time he, himself, has to spare from his other activi-
ties. What happens then? He is taught nothing, because he
cannot be taught anything. His mind is coloured by his own
worldly position and importance, congratulating itself on its
highly developed Western knowledge, against the standards
of which, indeed, he will insist on measuring all he hears. He
is graciously prepared to give the Teacher an opportunity of
proving his worth and will see if he approves of him and if he
is fit to teach such an one as himself. He returns to his own
land a sadder but no wiser man, because apparently these much
vaunted Teachers know nothing after all!

How then should he go? As Milarepa went, who understood the relationship and knew the infinite respect due to
such a Guru as Marpa. Not merely cap in hand did he go to
his selected Master, but on his knees he bowed down before
him with his head on the ground in humble obeisance—a
practice abhorrent to the Western mind. Instead of seeing if
the Teacher is sufficiently learned to be able to instruct him,
the would-be disciple must offer himself, 'body, mind and
speech', to the Master and be prepared to suffer anything at
his hands in order to obtain the Teaching finally when he is
ready for it. For he is aware that it is he, himself, and not the
Master who is on trial and who must prove himself worthy to
receive the Hidden Truth.

He must be prepared to spend his whole life, if necessary,
not merely a few months of vacation, in the pursuit of Knowledge. He must suffer and endure and count nothing of
greater value than the acquisition of these Truths. He must
be prepared to act as servant to his Master, for the chela is
always servant to his Guru, and to do the most menial tasks,
not when asked but spontaneously out of devotion and love
for him. He must forget any Western academic distinctions

4

he may have gained which are as nothing compared with the Initiations the Guru has received; the degrees after his name, his station in life or his age are of no importance and merely tend to keep the sense of values perverted. Implicit obedience to and complete trust in the Guru is also an essential requirement.

The chela has one right—to choose his Guru, and the Guru may accept or reject him at will; but once accepted, thereafter that chela belongs to his Master and is to him as a son and a servant with no right of reservation to decide any matter for himself. That is why his faith must be complete. Hence it is important that the aspirant does not fall for the mass charlatanry practised on the unsuspecting traveller by men with highly developed psychic powers and no corresponding spiritual evolution. But when he has found his Guru he gives himself wholly to him until his Search is over and the Truth attained—and when that will be depends on himself alone.

## HIGHER POWERS

The third point we have to make, therefore, concerns these Higher or Psychic Powers which the true Yogi can manifest privately to his disciples for their benefit, but which he never displays to a merely curious public, even when goaded by disbelief, nor for the purpose of gain. By this it is possible to distinguish between the truly evolved person, the Guru, and the charlatan-fakir or charlatan-Yogi. These psychic powers have been well attested down the centuries by responsible persons. They come with the practice of mind control and are known only in very attenuated forms in the West as 'natural gifts' in a few men and women, who may make a career for themselves as 'mediums' or else are so frightened of their abilities that they suppress them and prefer not even to think about them.

Let no one smile superiorly at the incidents recorded in the story of Milarepa's life, such as his ability to fly, to meditate without sleep, to accomplish a two months' journey in three days or to manifest himself in many places at the same time as he did on his last journey to Chobar. These and other still more extraordinary abilities can be developed by highly trained and self-disciplined Yogis whose power of Concentration is absolute. The altering of the pulse rate, the stopping of the heart-beat, the arrest of haemorrhage after a deliberately deep cut and the subsequent rapid healing of the wound, are phenomena which have been seen and studied by doctors of the West as well as the East, doctors who have come in doubt and left in wonder. Suspended animation, corresponding to animal hibernation, enables some to be buried alive and dug up again weeks, or even months after. This too has been witnessed by the profession as well as by Government officials and other responsible persons.

The generation of Vital Heat, known in Tibet as *Tum-mo*, which Milarepa was so anxious to achieve, is a well-known practice. Tibetan yogis can sit out on the snow, naked, and melt the snow around them by raising their own body temperature until they are perspiring freely. Indeed, ordinary deep concentration will, itself, bring a warm flush all over the body and sweat—but then the physiological effects of concentration and meditation have yet to be studied by the medical profession, interesting as they are and well-known to all who have begun to practise them. Telepathy is, of course, elementary in the spiritual or psychic growth and from it follows the power of deep perception by which the most hidden thoughts and motives of men can be known.

None of these abilities seem strange to the Easterner; he has been brought up on tales of such persons and has often seen the lower variety who seek money and fame by the display of their powers. It is only the Westerner who thinks his measuring rule, his scales and his microscope are reliable standards for judging Truth, who laughs at such stories and claims, forgetting that the more he relies on instruments the less will his own innate capacity have a chance of developing. The art of medicine of a century ago is now a science of medicine, with much loss both to patient and practitioner alike. The art of seamanship has become the science of navigation with every mechanical aid and the true sailor has almost disappeared. And now the art of being a man is becoming a science, too, and men will disappear from the face of the planet as have other species whose development became one-sided and ended in a cul-de-sac.

Let not the visiting Westerner expect—or worse still, ask—the great Guru or Great Lama to give a display of his powers for his benefit. He will deny having any. Everywhere in esoteric Teaching is the warning uttered against the powers being used either for gain or for proof of their possession. Let them not be pursued for their own sake, either, as some who come demand to be taught how to 'work miracles'. They come incidentally through the practice of meditation and mind control or not at all. The man or woman born clairvoyant or clairaudient or generally 'psychic' is but a freak of nature, a throw-back to a more 'primitive' age when the possession of these faculties was a property of the human race.

Those who display these powers for public admiration, it can be safely assumed, are not to be taken seriously as Gurus, nor to be regarded as anything but vain men of the world, even if they sit cross-legged and stark naked in the midst of a throng of fervent disciples. It is a different matter when a Guru displays his powers for the instruction and benefit of his

7

disciples, as did Marpa for Milarepa's benefit on the eve of his departure, and Milarepa for the benefit of his followers when his own death was approaching. To misuse such powers is to put one's spiritual development in jeopardy and to heap up bad karma for oneself.

## KARMA

It must have become obvious to the reader in the course of the story, that the Doctrine of Karma and that of Reincarnation, which are mutually dependent, are basic to the tale. Accepted in the East as a matter of course, it is only the Westerner brought up in the Christian tradition, or the Moslem following a similar one, to whom the idea seems both impossible and repulsive. Yet Christianity was five hundred years old before this belief was eradicated by papal decree as belonging to the Gnostic heresy. And there is evidence in the New Testament to suggest it was a commonly held idea of the Jewish people and one accepted by Christ. 'Who do men say that I am?' He asked His disciples one day. 'And they said: "Some say John the Baptist, some Elijah and others Jeremiah or one of the prophets" ' (Matt. xvi, 13; Mk. viii, 27). Or again—and even more significantly this time: '*If ye are willing to receive it*, this (John the Baptist) is Elijah that is to come. He that hath ears to hear let him hear' (Matt. xi. 14). There are eight references to John as the reincarnation of Elijah and they appear in all the gospels. But there is one further verse which shows that the disciples took the idea for granted: 'And as He passed by He saw a man blind from birth. And the disciples asked Him saying: "Rabbi, who did sin, this man or his parents that he should be born blind?" Jesus answered: "Neither did this man sin nor his parents . . ." ' (John. ix. 1–3), thus accepting the implication which He could have ridiculed of some previous

8

life—for how otherwise could a man sin before he was born?

However, Papal decree has done away successfully with a belief that could have a very definite moral effect; but it is still regarded in the East as a normal Law of Nature. The associated Doctrine of Karma is one of the main themes of this book and Milarepa often preached about it, since it was the idea of Karma that awoke him to the enormity of his own evil deeds in the practising of Black Magic and the destruction of so much life and property as the result. The treatment meted out to him by his Guru, which he bore so meekly and patiently, was suffering due to him for the suffering he had caused to others, if the matter is looked at in one way. Looked at from another angle it can be said that he had degenerated so far spiritually by his desire for procuring vengeance that he had 'to learn the hard way' before he could reach again the level at which he was born and develop on upward from there until he was at last fit to receive Instruction.

'As a man sows so also shall he reap' is one aspect of Karma, the one best known to the men of the West, but the effect of wrong-doing and wrong living also retards progressively the ability to receive the Teaching, so that the distance has to be made up again before one can start from scratch. Hence the working out of Karma is a perfectly natural Law and not to be interpreted as punishment administered by an angry God for man's sins.

No Karma can be elided or transferred to another, but good actions and good living can have its effect upon the spiritual growth, too, so that part of the distance may be made good without the whole space having to be traversed step by step. A close analogy will be found in the well-known children's game of Snakes and Ladders. The snake is the evil Karma accruing from an evil deed which puts the player back a certain distance so that he has to plod on again from the tail of the snake. But if he happens to arrive on a square which is the bottom of a ladder, he can rise abruptly for a certain distance, so that he has not had to cover every single square of the distance he lost. The ladder is the effect of good Karma from a good deed.

The Doctrine is one conducive to a higher morality than that which advertises a Mediator or Scapegoat for the sins of man, for so low are we in spiritual evolution that it is only the thought of punishment that deters us from even worse living than we normally engage in; and this 'bad living' also includes the doing of 'good works' when we have not sufficient realisation of the Truth to be able to do them with an utterly pure motive, as Milarepa points out in one of his last sermons.

Karma is a theme basic to the Buddhist Religion and Philosophy; but it was not invented by the Buddha, for it was part of Indian thought even before his age.

### FUNDAMENTAL PRINCIPLES OF BUDDHISM

When Milarepa recounts to his Guru, Marpa, the results of his eleven months of solitary meditation, what he states are the fundamental principles of Buddhism which he has not just learned academically but the significance of which he has been able to grasp with deep perception; for the perception gained by meditation is different from that which comes from ordinary study.

Seeing that non-Buddhist readers are probably unfamiliar even with the most basic principles of the Buddha's Teaching or history, the account of Milarepa's meditation will need to be set out more fully as, in effect, a brief and attenuated survey of the Dharma, the Doctrine the Buddha taught.

## Introduction

After some years of trying various paths, following different teachers and practising asceticism in its most stringent form, Gautama Siddartha (born in 563 B.C.), erstwhile wealthy young lordling who had given up every blessing that the world could bestow, came to a place in India called Gaya, and there he sat down under a *pipul* tree, making the granite resolve not to rise again until he had gained Enlightenment and known Reality as opposed to this world of phenomena. He had come to the conclusion that Meditation of the highest type was the only way. In the hours that followed he had to bear with the assaults of his own lower nature, as do all great Teachers on the eve of their final graduation from the material to the spiritual, and he did battle with himself, his desires and emotions, doubts and fears, pulling one way and his belief in his mission drawing him ever upward and away from them. Then towards dawn, conqueror of Himself, He gained Enlightenment and saw the world as it really was, and He rose from his seat—the Buddha.

Then He walked from Gaya to Saranath, near Benares, where He preached The First Sermon, still available to be read by those who wish to read it; in this He enunciated the Great Truths which He had discovered, or rather, those of them which ordinary men could understand—for who could comprehend Absolute Truth while still unenlightened?

Truth, when uttered, is received at different levels by its hearers according to the degree of their spiritual development. If it seems to be no Truth but an untruth, or if it appears trite, then the hearer may be sure the fault is in himself and not in the Truth. As he develops and meditates on it, more and more comes to be perceived in it; the triteness disappears, the profundity seems to grow. If he reaches the acme of spiritual development, as did the Buddha that night, then the profundity is seen to be infinite.

11

*The Life of Milarepa*

With this much warning, therefore, let us listen to the Truth given in that First Sermon in the Deer Park at Saranath.

## THE FOUR NOBLE TRUTHS

1. Suffering is a characteristic of Life on Earth.
2. The cause of suffering is Desire.
3. Cessation of Desire would procure cessation of suffering.
4. The means to that cessation is by the Noble Eightfold Path of Right Living.

These Truths, the Four Noble or Aryan Truths as they are always called, are not to be argued about but to be *plumbed*, and they go much deeper than appears on the surface and at first sight. Indeed, a lifetime of plumbing will continue to bear fruit.

## THE NOBLE EIGHTFOLD PATH

The Noble Eightfold Path comprises Right Viewpoint, Right Aim, Right Speech, Right Conduct, Right Livelihood, Right Effort, Right Mindfulness and Right Concentration.

Naturally each of these should be discoursed on separately, but suffice it to say that all the other seven depend on the first, Right Viewpoint, or The Right Sense of Values. So long as we hold the things of this world dear and do not realise their intrinsic worthlessness, despite what all the Master Teachers the world has received have unanimously said about them, so long will the need for altering our whole attitude to life go unrecognised and the need for self evolution and a religion which stresses it be ignored.

From another Discourse by the Buddha, comes His great

concept of the Wheel of Birth and Death, the hub of which is made up of Greed, Ignorance and Hatred—those common characteristics of the human race.

Ignorance—lack of knowledge of what is important and what is unimportant in the ultimate scheme of things—is the chief cause of the incessant round of births and deaths that human beings undergo—unless they obtain Buddhahood. Men are born again and again because they *want* to be born again and again, although they often do not realise it or would not admit it; because they are enamoured with the pleasures of the world, that are no real pleasures, and at the moment of their death they cling to life. Science calls it the Law of Self Preservation, and regards it as a Law of Nature, which it is not, unless the qualifying word 'Lower' is inserted before 'Nature'.

The twelve *'nidanas'* then mentioned by Milarepa are the twelve causes, or rather, interdependent connections, which form the run of the Wheel of Rebirth and Death, ever revolving and on which we come and go and come and go. . . . The nidanas are Ignorance—Karma formation—consciousness—mind-body—sense organs—contact—sensation—craving—attachment—coming-to-be—birth—suffering, old age, death.

Being circular one can start at any point of the wheel and see how all are inextricably mixed up. They are not causes in the mechanical senses, but interdependencies. Nothing stands alone in its own right unrelated to anything else. Hence nothing is Real for all is relative. Reality is unsupported identity—the Absolute. When a man reaches Buddhahood and gains Enlightenment, he fully comprehends the fallacy of the subject-object relationship, the unreal relationship which not only does not correspond to Truth but impedes the apprehension of it. He sees that 'I and the rest' is a wrong basis for thinking, and from this he understands the non-existence of 'I' at all, which is as much interdependent and relative as

13

anything else in the world despite our fixed and basic belief to the contrary.

Out of this arises the famous Buddhist Doctrine of the non-existence of the soul, of a permanent 'I'. For, Buddha maintained, the 'I' was no more permanent or unchanging than a river. What went on from life to life and through life, was a bundle of Karmic effects made up of the 5 *skandhas*, or aggregates: body, feeling, perception, tendencies (or volition) and consciousness. As the result of our mode of living, for better or for worse, so these aggregates change during our life and what is reborn is no more the same thing that died than is the river at any point the same river into which you can step twice. It has a general identity in virtue of which it is called the Ganges or the Thames, but not a particular one, because its content of water and bed of stones is ever changing. So my Karmic effects have an identity which distinguishes them from your Karmic effects, but they have not the particular identity which my persistent use of the word 'I' would suggest.

One who attains Enlightenment merges with the Absolute and therefore is aware of the oneness of all, as the result of which any subject–object basis for thought is seen to be wrong thinking and unproductive of Truth. To strive to gain this comprehension of the non-existence or unreality of the Self in the face of every feeling to the contrary, is the aim ·of Right Living, of the Eightfold Path. And when that is achieved, naturally all self-seeking, all pride, all hatred and a wrong sense of values is obliterated. By following the Eightfold Path and by the practice of Meditation—the one useless without the other—the Path to Enlightenment opens to us. Indeed, life has been given as a means to attain this realisation and our bodies are vehicles for this purpose alone—another Truth Milarepa grasps and enunciates to his Master.

To set foot on the Eightfold Path, Milarepa recognised that

*Introduction*

two things were necessary: Refuge in the Triple Gem and a Guru. The Triple Gem is the name given to the Trinity of the Buddha (or Buddhahood), the Dharma and the Sangha (that body of men who has realised Buddhahood in the past and who will realise it in the future, the Bodhisattvas and Arahants (see below)), and taking Refuge in the Triple Gem and the acceptance of the Five Precepts is the outward affirmation of the Buddhist, whether for the first time as a convert or periodically afterwards as a practising devotee. By 'taking Refuge' is meant accepting the Buddha as a Master-Teacher, accepting the Dharma as the Truth realised and taught by Him, which is to be put into practice in everyday life, and the Sangha as a shining example of ordinary human beings who have achieved the purpose of their existence. (They correspond roughly to the Saints of the Christian Church.)

The Five Precepts the layman takes are against Killing, Stealing, Adultery, Lying and Intoxicating Drink. The sramanera when ordained takes Ten Precepts, adding five, and they are reaffirmed when he is given his Higher Ordination to become a fully fledged bhikku or mendicant monk (gelong). Above these are the rules of the Bodhisattva Vow which only those who have set foot on the Path of the Bodhisattva, take. This rather than the Precepts is referred to by Milarepa in his conversation with the Geshé's mistress.

It has been necessary in this brief survey to go beyond what Milarepa discovered in order to make the view of Buddhist principles to some degree comprehensive, although naturally justice can in no way be done to the Teaching. But the fundamentals, if no more, are here and it is worthwhile deviating a little to embrace them, since the Buddha went further than philosopher or metaphysician since has gone, and His philosophical system is well worth studying by those who are still puzzling over the problems of the Western school, which have

15

not been resolved since they were first propounded by Plato and Aristotle. It was the enunciation of such principles as these that laid Him open apparently even in His own lifetime, and certainly since, to the charge of negativism and pessimism by those who could not see the profundity of the Teaching and looked merely at the surface.

What follows in Milarepa's account of his meditational exercises necessitates now a brief glance at the three great sects of Buddhism, sects which are not mutually exclusive as are the sects of Christianity but which resulted from the development of different emphasis within the framework of the same Dharma. These three are the Hinayana (also known as the Lesser Vehicle or Path and referred to as such by Milarepa), which is commonly found in Southern countries, Ceylon, Burma, Laos and Thailand; the Mahayana (or Great Vehicle or Path) of the North of India, Tibet, Mongolia and China; and the Tantrayana (or the Way of Tantra) in Tibet, erroneously termed Lamaism.

The Hinayana school adhered very strictly to the letter of the law, and in this school of thought developed the theory of the Arahant who gains Enlightenment for himself alone and who then departs into Nirvana, never to be born again, and leaves the rest of humanity to fend for itself. This aspiration, it will be remembered, was roundly condemned by Milarepa, as it is by all Mahayanists. Did not the Buddha send out His disciples to preach as soon as they had won Enlightenment? The Mahayana school, therefore, stressed the idea of the Bodhisattva, who seeks Enlightenment, not for himself alone, but in order to be able to teach the masses of the people still left in the darkness of ignorance. And for this purpose he renounces his chance of entering Nirvana; that is, he postpones his own final emancipation for the sake of others. It is the point that Milarepa stresses again and again in his dis-

16

courses: 'He who seeks only his own freedom and happiness takes the Lower Path, but he who feels love and Compassion to other beings so that he wants to help them towards Emancipation too, he has set foot on the Higher Path and to take to the Higher one must know exactly where one is going and what is the goal' (p. 83).

It was the necessity of acquiring knowledge of the goal which the Bodhisattva has to do again at each rebirth, that gave Milarepa his last realisation that a Guru is needed for the attainment of Enlightenment. Indeed, it is commonly asserted that the Dharma must be studied at the feet of a Master and the Master, like Marpa, must have the power to know what line of Teaching will be most suited to the chela, for this differs with the individual. 'One must experience the Truth, not merely have an academic acquaintance with it. And neither bodily comfort nor even bodily necessities should be allowed to stand in the way; every obstacle must be surmounted and every sacrifice, even life itself, must be willingly made.'

Bodhisattvas may, of course, be at different stages of development, but their outstanding characteristic is awareness of a purpose in their incarnation and a desire to learn in order to Teach. Those of the highest order are such as attain to Buddhahood (and some would add, to Christhood, as being synonymous) in their final life after many lives devoted to the service of others. The stories of the Buddha's previous incarnations as a Bodhisattva over long aeons of time, show this clearly, and recollection of some if not all of their previous incarnations is a sign in men of higher development.

In the table given at the beginning of the chapter, it will be seen that the word 'Rimpoche' has been given as the equivalent of 'Bodhisattva'. In Tibet there is a whole class of persons who are 'Real Incarnations' or recognised as being great

Lamas who have died. They are discovered by the same process as is the Dalai Lama. Certain unusual features may
accompany a birth or a small child may be out of the ordinary
in its behaviour. Certain articles which belonged to the dead
person whose reincarnation the boy may be, are shown to him
along with identical imitations and the child has to choose
those which were once his own accurately. Other tests may
also be given. When the examiners are satisfied, the parents
are persuaded to relinquish him and he is put into a monastery
for intensive training, usually the one which he was supposed
to have occupied before. His education is overseen with far
greater intensity and strictness than that of the rest of the
novices, and despite this, he is given special preferential treatment in certain respects and every respect must always be
shown to him. But daily from the age of eight he has to learn
by heart, and he may not play with other children and beatings are frequent and severe, both to counteract laziness and
that he may experience suffering.

It is through this system that so many of the big monasteries
in Tibet are ruled by very young men hardly out of boyhood,
for they are the recognised Incarnations of previous Abbots.
The term 'Rimpoche' does not mean 'Bodhisattva' but is a
title of respect always given to Real Incarnations and hence
has become substituted for the other. Sometimes a Rimpoche
will resist all persuasion to take monkhood and return, after
his education is finished, to the world of laymen. He may,
however, be empowered to give Initiations and be a Lama
though married and carrying on a business. To this class
Marpa and Ngogdun-Chudor belonged; nor is it recorded
that Milarepa himself ever became a gelong, but from his
history it seems that he took the Precepts of the genyen and
had his head shaved and donned the genyen's robes.

(It may interest the reader to know that the Real Incarnation of Rechung, the original author of the biography of Milarepa, is now resident in India, driven, like so many other Lamas and Rimpoches, from his home in Tibet by the Communist aggression.)

In the Tantrayana, which grew out of the Mahayana, just as the Mahayana grew out of the Hinayana, emphasis shifted to the use of the body for the development of the mind and to the valuable aid which can be given by occult means. The oft-referred-to Initiations are of this order. Only a Guru empowered to Initiate can do so successfully and the higher he is developed spiritually the better is he able to pass on the Power to the Initiate. This has to be implanted into the mind of the candidate who must, however, be ready to receive it; indeed, if he is not, he will not receive it even if it is bestowed with all the attendant rites.

There are two other points that may puzzle the non-Buddhist reader: the Doctrine of the Void, referred to by Milarepa several times in his songs during his death and cremation, and the frequent references to the 'gods', since even the most ignorant know that Buddhism is supposed to be an atheistic religion and that the Buddha, it is said, denied the existence of a God.

The Doctrine of the Void is impossible to explain briefly or simply. Indeed, in the taking of the Bodhisattva Vow one of the rules the Bodhisattva has to keep in mind thereafter is not to expound the Doctrine of the Void to those not yet ready for it. For it is the peak of Buddhist metaphysics and must be *felt* rather than reasoned about. But even referring to it one must bring in the other concept—that of the Absolute. For the Buddha, far from denying that there was an Absolute, asserted that those who reached Enlightenment might merge with It and so perceive Reality as opposed to the world of illusion and phenomenon. What He did say, however, which has led to the charge of atheism being levelled against Him, is that we have no means of expressing anything whatever about It. Words belong to the phenomenal universe and are applicable only to that. When one goes beyond the phenomenal to Reality, words must perforce be left behind. No teaching, no description, no thought can deal with the Absolute—but we can *experience* It if sufficiently evolved.

What the Buddha combated was the numerous attempts that had been made, were being made and would in the future be made, to say that the Absolute was this or that, a personal God, a Creator, a Father-God. He persistently refused to answer any questions about the matter because it was inexpressible in words. He was not going to allow his disciples to imagine an Absolute in their own image, as is the tendency of man everywhere. And He made the subtle point that it is better to set about trying to win Enlightenment and therefore have experience of the Absolute oneself, than to waste time trying ineffectually to talk about It, when nothing which can be said about it can possibly be *absolutely* true. Words would inevitably modify It and push It into their mould and would so give, at the best, a rough approximation. The words may be true at a certain level but only at a level and so will only be relative Truth. Moreover, how can an understanding which can only function through the medium of words comprehend that which cannot be put into words? Only by experiencing It.

If this fact had been assimilated at the expense of human pride, there would have been less bigotry and so less violence and suffering committed in the name of religion, between all the various adherents to their own beliefs; all of whom assert confidently and dogmatically that they, only, have been given the Truth and that all others are wrong and must be saved from their wilful ignorance.

*Introduction*

The Absolute as a Creator may be a relative Truth, true at a certain level, but it must be realised that in the realm of the Absolute it is nearer the Truth to understand that when the Absolute creates then the Absolute *is* the Creation; that the cause of the thing is the thing itself and that our idea of causation is purely a pragmatic one, depending as it does on succession in time and proximity in space. But neither Time nor Space are ideas applicable to the Absolute. Yet even here we are going beyond what it is possible or permissible to assert, for we are making certain assertions concerning the Absolute which again are only relatively true; but the level of atemporal and aspatial *acausal* causality is a little higher than that of pragmatic causation.

The Doctrine of the Void is, then, a denial of the Reality of the world of Sense Perception. Even the term 'Void' is misleading, for it suggests Empty Space and Space, too, must be eliminated as being virtually non-existent. Nirvana is said to be the Void, so also is Samsara, the phenomenal world, and the two are not two but one. Nevertheless, one should spend one's life struggling to rise above Samsara and reach Nirvana —the Law of Contradiction, like the other two Laws of Thought in Formal Logic, not being applicable to Thought above a certain low level, the level at which we think normally.

This is the major contribution which the Buddha made to metaphysics and in doing so He abolished the problems that the Western philosophers from the time of Plato and Aristotle on, have still been thinking and writing about, all unaware of the advancement in the Search for Truth made in India when Plato was still an infant which annihilated those problems. Yet even to-day paper and ink are spent on them.

If, then, there is no God in the sense of a personal God, or if it is realised that concepts of a personal God, a Creator or a

C21

Father-God are only relatively true and suited to certain stages in human development, why are there so many references to the 'gods', suggestive of a whole hierarchy?

The Pali word *'deva'* is translated 'god', but really means 'spirit' a Being from a Higher Plane which, in Buddhist thought, can influence human beings and help and protect them. This Earth is not the only world of beings in Buddhist cosmology. There are countless Universes on different planes of existence, i.e. at different stages of (spiritual) evolution; some are higher than ours, the majority; some are lower; many are the references to beings—human beings—being born again in a higher or a lower world.

But in Buddhism there is no place for the massive hierarchy of the Hindu religion, which added the Buddha Himself to this hierarchy, even as the Christians made Him into one of their Saints; nor for the Trinity of Creator, Preserver, Destroyer, nor for anything except an unmentionable Absolute towards which or away from which people are evolving, some having become spirits on a higher plane and some having sunk to lower worlds. Yet all belong to the world of phenomena, none to Reality. Only the Absolute is Real and we cannot even really say that about It without stating something less than the Truth. But It is there to be realised by one and all who have the desire and determination of a Milarepa, for it is the belief that, just as it is said that every army private has a field marshal's baton in his kitbag, so every human being —every being—is a potential Buddha. It is up to him to actualise Buddhahoo⌐ in himself.

\*          \*          \*

This is a very inadequate sketch of Buddhism merely intended for those who are wholly ignorant of the religion and philosophy of the Buddha. Anyone interested could do no better than to read that masterly work, *Survey of Buddhism*, by Bhikshu Sangharakshita, at once a readable and a scholarly book, published by the Indian Institute of World Culture.

There is a final, lesser, question that may arise in the mind of the reader, concerning the reputed bad temper of Marpa. Naturally a man who is very highly developed should have no temper because it would have been so habitually subdued. At one point he—or Rechung—goes to some trouble to point out that his outbursts were not of the ordinary variety but were displays of 'religious temper', put on purely for the benefit of his pupils. Against this, however, is Mrs Marpa's story that her parents gave her a turquoise before her marriage, so that she should not be destitute if she found life unbearable with one whose irascibility was so notorious. There is no way of deciding the point and the reader must make up his own mind for himself.

At all events his so-called bad temper gives even more emphasis to the chela–Guru relationship already dealt with. As Marpa himself says, he has the right to cut Milarepa up into little bits and no one could properly stop him—not that any Guru would do such a thing, of course. But, on the other hand, there is certainly no question of any chela bringing an action for assault against his Guru (as many a modern school child does against his schoolmaster after just punishment), if beaten or knocked down. This would be utterly contrary to the recognised relationship and the trust in the Guru necessary for that successful relationship. Marpa, as it turned out, seems to have known exactly what he was doing in the case of Milarepa and to have acted for the best. It is for the chela to put his desire for the Truth, which can only be obtained from the Guru, before all bodily comfort and dignity which are of small importance in comparison.

There is a story in Buddhist literature of a disciple who

stated that he wanted the Truth more than anything else. His Guru took him by the scruff of his neck and held his head down in the river until he was nearly drowned. When he released him he asked him: 'What did you want most of all when your head was under water?' 'Air,' gasped the chela. 'When you want Truth as much as that, you will be ready to be taught,' said the Guru.

Let those who come from the West to the East, therefore, in search of a Guru and the Teaching, remember that sincerity of purpose and an unshakeable determination is the first essential. The Eastern Guru tends to regard the Western aspirant with suspicion, from bitter experience, and would rather avoid contact, simply because the chela–Guru relationship is neither understood nor held in any respect when it is explained by other pupils. Thus the really sincere Seeker has to suffer for the behaviour of all the rest who come with the idea that the Teaching is to be bought with money and that 'he who pays the piper calls the tune'. By such the story of Milarepa can never be read too often.

# I

# His Birth and Early Years

My name is Rechung and I am a disciple of Jetsun Milarepa, the most renowned Yogi of all time and my beloved Master. Shortly before his death, as the result of a vision I had while meditating one evening, I begged him to tell us the story of his life, and in this I was backed by the other disciples, all of whom knew a little but longed to hear a detailed account, for there were many lessons to be learned from a history such as his; and I engaged to listen attentively and to write down each day what we had heard, that the world might be a richer place as the result of learning of his sufferings and triumphs, his knowledge and achievements.

It was already common property how he had practised the Black Arts in his adolescence and early manhood for the punishment of his enemies, who, it may be said, justly deserved all they received; how, thereafter, stricken by remorse and truly desiring to learn the Truth, he had endured such physical and mental sufferings in the pursuance of his quest as would have turned aside lesser mortals, but by perseverance and refusal to admit defeat had finally triumphed; how he then retired from the world into a hermitage in order to develop his knowledge so hardly acquired within himself; and how, towards the end of his life, he had devoted himself to the saving of as many beings as would listen to him, of whom I was one.

So much we knew, but how much more there was to tell!

The Life of Milarepa

With what details did he gladden our hearts and by what wealth of expression did he bring tears to our eyes! How we smiled at his whimsical anecdotes and how intently did we listen to every word he uttered that none should be lost! And how unworthy am I to set down what my Master said—and yet how privileged too!

What you will read here is factual, the story of a man who started life just like one of ourselves, but who ended it—oh, how different! Few there are who attain to the Highest Powers and win control first of their very Selves and then of the elements and Beings of other spheres, or who comprehend completely the true nature of the Universe and the unity of everything therein; for this is Enlightenment. Few there are who persevere in the face of apparently insuperable obstacles. Few there are who sin so grievously and yet retrieve what they have done and rise above their just rewards.

Milarepa did just this; Milarepa who was my Master when in the flesh and who is still my master, though his body is now but a heap of ashes. To you, then, Great Guru, I make obeisance and may this history find favour in your sight! Speak now and let the world hear!

\*     \*     \*

My magical powers I must have inherited from my ancestors for they seem to have been a characteristic of our family. Five generations back a forebear of mine made a name for himself, literally, by exorcising a demon whom no other magician could dislodge. It is said that the demon ran away from him in terror crying: 'Mi.la! Mi.la!' 'O Man! O Man!' as the result of which folks began jokingly to call him Mila and the name stuck so well that it became handed down from father to son, attached to their other names.

When I was born my father was so delighted to hear the
26

## His Birth and Early Years

news that I was called Thöpaga, meaning 'Delightful to Hear', which turned out singularly appropriate as I was gifted with a fine singing voice. However, I anticipate a little and must return first to my ancestors, so that you can see the nature of our family circumstances at the time of my father's premature death.

The son of Mila the Exorcist was an inveterate gambler, sometimes lucky but a little too sure of himself, with the result that the entire family fortunes disappeared one night, falling to a sharper player than himself, who scooped our houses, furniture, jewels and lands into his bag and took possession while my great-grandfather, a sadder if not a wiser man, had to take to the road with his son, Dorje Sengé, and make what living he could in the practice of preventing hailstorms, which did so much damage to people's crops, manufacturing charms for children and also exorcising spirits wherever they might be troubling village folk.

Dorje Sengé was, however, of a more practical turn of mind, and began trading in wool so that in a comparatively short space of time he managed to recoup his father's losses and re-establish him as one of the landed gentry with a house and farms to hand down to his heirs, of which I was ultimately one. The house he built for himself was a large and magnificent structure supported on four columns and eight pillars and three storeys high, thus deserving the name of 'Four and Eight', by which it was henceforth known.

His wealth steadily increased and his prosperity attracted certain of his poor relations, who left their own part of the country and came and settled near him in our province of Kyang Tsa, with their few possessions and their children—an event which was to have no small effect on our lives, in due course turning bliss into tragedy.

My father was Mila Sharab Gyalten and my mother's name

27

was Karmo Kyen, or White Garland, and she gave birth to
me on August 25 in the year of the Male Water Dragon
(A.D. 1052). Four years later she presented me with a little
sister who was named Gonkyit, a word too hard for my baby
tongue so that we all called her by the pet name of Peta.

How happy we were in those days as she and I romped
together in the house and fields, decked out in jewels and carefully tended, in fine clothes and with plenty to eat and drink,
blissful in our unawareness of what lay ahead of us. And how
the neighbours used to envy us and speak in awed whispers
whenever they came to our home, gazing at the furnishings
and ornaments in respectful wonder and bowing low to our
parents whenever they chanced to meet them. And I was
already betrothed to a little girl called Zesay, but in those days
I cared nought for that, preferring my games and my sister.

Peta was three and I was seven when my father took ill and
after a short period of suffering he died, entrusting his family to
the care of two of our poor relations, my Uncle and Aunt,
together with the property which was to be held and worked
in trust for us until I was grown up and able to manage our
affairs for myself. At the time of his illness my father was
indeed a wealthy man and much revered by the community,
most of whom were his tenants. All these and his kinsfolk he
called to his bedside so that they might hear and bear witness
to his last will and testament before he died and would know
what he had determined for his wife and children; it was as
if he wished to ensure protection against any possible mal-
practices on the part of his near relations whom, it seems,
he did not wholly trust.

How right he was, so it turned out! For on the day of the
funeral, when his body was no more, the neighbours all
gathered together in our garden and some of our distant
cousins suggested that my mother should run the estate and

receive help how and when she needed it. But my Uncle and
Aunt promptly intervened, pointing out that they had been
left sole guardians as the only near relatives, so that they intended to do as they liked with the property and needed advice
from no one. They would, of course, care for the widow and
orphans.

What an overstatement that was! Far from caring for us,
Peta and I were soon wandering around in rags, hungry and
dirty, forced to work in the fields in the summer for Uncle and
in the house in the winter for Aunt, who cared nothing for our
blisters or sores, nor even for the lice which quickly infested
our unwashed bodies and tattered clothes. Some of the neighbours pitied us and might even weep at the sight we presented,
but others, the time-servers, made up to Uncle and Aunt, who
were now the wealthy and fortunate ones, and lords of the
manor, as it were. They might be seen, indeed, in our parents'
clothes and jewellery, for they had divided up the small stuff
between them, ignoring my mother's claim to what had been
her own, so that now they were able to appear decked out in
keeping with the new station in life to which they had pro-
moted themselves. Further, the time-servers began to criticise
my mother, whom they had previously respected so highly,
and called her weak and helpless and an able housewife only
when supported by a strong and prosperous husband.

Zesay's parents were among those who were kind and who
pitied our miserable condition, giving a few of the necessities
of life to us children now and again; and they impressed on me
the first lesson Life has to teach everyone: how unstable and
impermanent is property; like the dew on the grass, here now
and gone in the next hour. And then they would comfort me
by assuring me that I, too, like my great-grandfather, would
one day acquire wealth again.

For eight years my mother endured the gossiping and

29

innuendoes of the neighbours, but at last, when I was fifteen years old, she tried to resist. She had a field of her own which annually brought in a small income and which was managed by her brother, a secret sympathiser, but, as will be seen, one who had not the courage of his convictions. This year she decided to give a feast with the entire proceeds of the harvest and to invite all the village as well as our relatives, and demand the inheritance on my behalf. To this end Peta and I worked hard scrubbing and cleaning and preparing the food and drink, borrowing utensils and trappings from our friends. When the great day arrived, the guests gathered, among them the delinquent couple themselves, who were given preferential treatment and the choicest morsels. When all had eaten and the beer was freely flowing my mother rose and going into the midst of the company she brandished our father's last will and testament and asked her brother to read it out aloud to all to refresh their memories as to its contents. Afterwards she skilfully thanked our Uncle and Aunt for having looked after things so well and then, coming to the crucial point, demanded that now I, her son, was nearly grown, it was time that the inheritance was handed over to me to manage and the guardianship surrendered.

We saw the flushes of anger rise on the faces of our persecutors, who, although normally they never agreed about anything, now showed a united front in running down the proposition and scouting it as an utter absurdity if not almost an immoral suggestion. They even had the temerity to suggest that the house and land really belonged to them all the time and that our father had borrowed all that he had from them, though how anyone could believe such an impudent claim I cannot see. They added a few succinct remarks on the ingratitude of those whom they had saved for so long from starvation and gave final force to their words by administering some hard slaps on my mother's face; while Peta and I did not get off unscathed. This was too much for Mother who burst into hysterical weeping and then sank upon the floor in a faint. My mother's brother rose to his feet but feared to intervene for it would have meant he would have to take on the numerous stalwart sons of his opponent. Such as the neighbours as were in sympathy with us, set about reviving Mother, but Aunt had not yet finished with us. At the gate she turned and delivered herself of this parting invective:

'Here you are demanding wealth and you can afford to give a great party like this,' she screamed: 'We could not! Orphans! Huh! Don't think you will ever get another penny from us, do what you will! Fight us or curse us; we don't care! *Good* day to you!' And with that the pair of them stamped off with all the time-servers, leaving us with our handful of friends.

These soon found consolation in what was left of the beer, and over their mugs they proposed to raise a subscription for my education; our other uncle offered to take Mother and Peta into his own house in return for their working in the fields. But Mother still had her pride left and preferred to stay on her own smallholding, while accepting the proffered subscription for my education, which, up till then, had naturally been badly neglected.

Shortly after this memorable day, therefore, I was packed off to a private tutor, a Lama of some repute, while Mother and Peta continued to live and work, supported in various ways by our good uncle and his family, so that at least they did not have to go a-begging. Zesay, too, and her parents helped where they could, and often she was allowed to come and visit me and bring me little presents. Still, our clothes were ragged and our fare coarse and scanty, so that within me there grew up a great resentment against the cause of our unnecessary suffering.

II

# The Art of Black Magic

A few years passed thus, then one day my preliminary school-
ing came to an abrupt end.

My tutor, who was popular as a schoolmaster, was invited
one day to attend a feast in his honour in the village. The
drink flowed freely and he partook without restraint. He had
taken me with him to attend upon him, and I, too, became a
little tipsy. On the way home, full of the good things of life
and loaded with my master's presents, for I had been sent on
ahead with them, I felt the urge to raise my voice in song,
liking the sound of it very much; and so it happened that I was
singing away merrily when passing my mother's smallholding
en route for my tutor's place. My mother, who was roasting
barley inside the house, could not fail to recognise the sweet
strains of my voice, yet she was incredulous for she could not
conceive of my having found anything to be merry about,
considering our circumstances.

As soon as her eyes had confirmed the witness of her ears
she dropped the tongs from her right hand and the roasting
whisk from her left and, seizing a handful of ashes and a rod,
she came running out of the house, threw the ashes into my
face without hesitation and then proceeded to beat me about
the head with the stick, the while invoking my dead father to
look down and see what a worthless son he had begotten,
until, all of a sudden overcome, she fell down in a faint.

32

Peta, who had heard the commotion, cried out to me: 'What are you thinking of, brother? Do something about Mother, quickly!' and then she burst into tears. This, together with the beating, had a sobering effect upon me, and she and I tried to bring our mother round, slapping her hands and calling to her. As soon as she did revive she sat up and scolded me roundly for my merriment:

'Son, what have you got to be so cheerful about that you can come here singing? To my mind we are the most unhappy family in the world and I can do nothing but weep for our misery.' By this time we were all three of us in tears.

Then I said: 'Mother, you are quite right. But do not worry any more. I will do anything you want me to, I swear. What would you like me to do, Mother?'

To which Mother replied: 'I should like to see you dragging our enemies in the dust, but that is not possible. Still the next best thing is to go and learn Black Magic and then you can kill them safely, especially your Uncle and Aunt, who have treated us so badly, and wipe out the whole brood that none survive. Try and see if you can do this for me.'

'If you can give me the Teacher's fees,' I said, 'I will certainly do what you ask. I shall also need something for travelling expenses and maintenance though.'

This was no obstacle to my mother's resolve, for she promptly bartered one half of her field for a turquoise ring and a white pony, and managed also to collect two loads of madder dye and two of unrefined sugar, which latter I sold and so had enough for the road. Therefore, loading the pony I set forth and put up at an inn in Gungthang called The Inn of Self-Perfection, where I stayed to find someone else who was going my way for company. Here I met five young gentlemen, all anxious to learn the Black Arts, and we agreed to go on together; but first my mother, who had come so far with

33

me, took them aside and confided to them that I was something of a wastrel and would they please see that I attended to
my studies and keep my nose to the grindstone.

Going some way with us she provided us at our halts with
beer, but at last the time came when she had to leave us.
Mother broke down, and sobbing her farewell said to me:
'Remember our condition and work hard. You must become
able to wreak vengeance and destroy those who did the mischief. Your companions will be studying for the winning of
fame, you from sheer necessity. If you come back unable to
display your Black Magic, I shall kill myself here in front of
you.'

Greatly moved because I knew that she meant what she
said, I too shed tears and, promising faithfully that I would do
as she desired, said, 'Goodbye.'

In due course, having exchanged pony and dyestuff for
gold coins, I and my friends reached the place where the
Teacher of Black Magic lived, and to him I offered and
presented all I had, including my body and service in exchange
for his lore and my maintenance during the time it would take
me to learn all I needed to know.

The Lama smiled and accepted me, and so we began our
studies, continuing them for about a year. By this time my five
companions, well satisfied with what they had learned, were
dismissed with the present of a fine coat apiece. But although
the matters that we had been taught had many high-sounding
titles, I did not feel that I had achieved my purpose or touched
on more than the fringe of the subject. So I decided to return
and request further instruction, to which end I folded the coat
he had given me neatly to give it back to my Guru as a present,
it being all I had to bestow.

On the way back up the drive to the house, however, I
collected some manure and with this manured his garden, not

34

knowing he was watching me from a window; and I learned later from another pupil that he had remarked on what a kind, affectionate fellow I was, and how industrious, which then encouraged me very much. My Teacher greeted me kindly and asked why I wanted to learn more, so I poured out the full tale of my family's sufferings. This so moved him with pity that he acceded to my request, although telling me that he had turned away many rich applicants who had brought invaluable gifts. He did take the precaution, however, of sending a disciple to make inquiries in my village to confirm the truth of my story, but when he was assured of it he sent for me and said:

'I did not teach you all I knew before because I did not know whether you would act stupidly and without sufficient cause. But now I am satisfied and will give you the whole teaching. Only for the next step you must go to an ex-pupil of mine in the Tsangpo Valley, who is a physician and Professor of Tantricism. He is skilled in the launching of hailstorms and in guiding them with his finger-tips, and I will give you a letter of recommendation and the necessary gifts and send my son with you as a guide. He and I have a pact: whoever comes to me wanting to learn how to deal death and destruction I send to my friend, and whoever comes to him wanting to know how to make hailstorms he sends on to me.'

Thus it was that we arrived at the residence of my new Teacher, who greeted us with obvious pleasure and instructed me to build myself a hermitage, small and strong, where I was to be immured while I practised his lessons; this completed, I spent a fortnight in the study of dealing destruction from a distance. At the end of this time I had a vision in which a goddess appeared and laid thirty-five bleeding heads at my feet. Next morning my Teacher came and told me that there were two more persons to be sacrificed, did I want them killed

35

or not? As these two were my Uncle and Aunt I said I wanted them spared that I might gloat over their misery, so when the time came to avenge our wrongs these two were saved.

And now I will tell you just how our revenge occurred.

Aunt and Uncle's eldest son was to be married and many guests were gathered at the house for the wedding; others were still on their way there, being less enthusiastic over going, since they had been sympathisers with us. They were talking together over the chances of my having as yet learned enough of the Black Arts to take vengeance and they were saying that even if I were unable to do anything, it was surely time that *Karma* overtook the wicked pair. These people had just come in sight of the house when I launched my powers. And this is what happened:

A maidservant was coming out of the house to draw water from the well and as she passed the stable she saw, to her horror, instead of ponies, great spiders, snakes and scorpions, one gigantic scorpion being apparently engaged in tugging at the central supporting pillar of the house. She screamed and her terror communicated itself to the ponies that were tethered below the house. They took fright and breaking their halters, stampeded, one colt crashing against the pillar with such force that it snapped. Down came the house in ruins, burying the thirty-five guests; their bodies lay beside those of the horses smothered in the debris, from which a great cloud of dust arose.

The noise of the crash and the cry that went up from those who had been forced to witness the tragedy, brought Peta out to investigate, and on seeing what had occurred she called excitedly to our mother:

'Quick, Mother, come and see. Auntie's house has fallen down and a lot of people have been killed!'

Mother, unable to believe her ears, came running out and as

she gazed on the destruction over which the dust cloud was now settling, she burst out into what can only be described as a paean of joy, calling on all the bystanders to witness the handiwork of her most worthy son and ending with these words: 'What a cheering sight my son has given me! What a blessing in my old age! Surely all our sorrows have been worth it for this! How glad I am to have lived to see such a day! Never has there been a happier moment in all my life!'

Now some of the neighbours, hearing this, thought she was justified, but others felt she went too far in gloating thus over the fallen and these would have seized her and tortured her for a witch, but they were restrained when reminded that what the son had done before he could do again, if anyone offended him; it was advised that I should be sought out and killed first, as only then would it be safe to bring my mother to book.

Uncle, who, with Aunt, had escaped unscathed from the ruins, was all for attacking Mother and killing her with his own bare hands, but he was restrained by the villagers who were not anxious for any further disaster to overtake them, and they told him outright that he was as much to blame as anyone for the state of things. They then put their heads together to form a plot to murder me. Meanwhile our other uncle, Mother's brother, roundly scolded my mother in no uncertain terms for having so freely expressed her feelings in public, and he warned her to keep her doors bolted and barred.

The maidservant who had escaped being killed, and who had previously been in our service in the days of our prosperity, sent a message on the quiet to Mother, warning her of the danger in which I stood, and she begged her to pass on the warning to me. Mother then sold the other half of her field

D                                37

and was wondering whom she could entrust with the money she wanted to send me, when a pilgrim came to her door begging. By inviting him to stay for a few days and weighing him up, she decided that he would be a safe person to entrust with a message to me, so she fed him well and gave him some small necessities.

Now the beggar had an old blanket cloak, badly in need of repair; this Mother took, ostensibly to mend, and she sewed the gold into a patch and on top of it sewed another patch which was black and then embroidered a constellation on it. She gave the cloak back to the pilgrim and with the added incentive of a handsome present, she asked him to carry a letter to me, telling him where to find me. Thereafter, with great cunning she told Peta to tell everybody that the pilgrim had brought a letter from me, going to the length of forging one herself, and finally it was given to her brother to show to people. In it she had made me seem to write boastfully of my powers, and utter threats against all who plotted to harm us.

This cooled the ardour of the conspirators who, indeed, in their terror, persuaded Uncle to restore to Mother a small portion of my patrimony, a field called Worma Triangle, which made up for what she had had to sell in order to furnish me with money.

The pilgrim managed to find me after some hunting and gave me welcome news of my mother and sister and also the letter which was, however, so cautiously worded that its meaning was completely lost on me, or at least that part of it which referred to the hidden money. For she first congratulated me and told me the story of the disaster and begged me to launch a hailstorm next, to destroy the crops of those of our neighbours who wished us ill, and she warned me of the plot afoot against my life. Then came the part of which I could make neither head nor tail: 'Should you be short of money,'

38

she had written, 'search for a valley facing north, hidden by a black cloud and lit by the Pleiades. There you will find seven of our relatives. They will provide you with all you need. Should you fail to find the valley, this pilgrim messenger lives there. Do not ask anybody else about it.'

This was a fine riddle! I knew nothing of valleys or relatives who might live in them, nor was the pilgrim able to answer any of my questions concerning it, but appeared as mystified as I was myself. So I decided to show the letter to my Teacher, who commented on the vindictiveness of my mother, wanting hailstorms after vengeance had already been wreaked, but neither could he throw any light upon the riddle. Not so his wife whose woman's wit readily solved it and with apparent ease!

She proceeded to call the pilgrim and after studying him a while she lit a huge fire and gave him beer to drink, the while playfully removing his cloak and pirouetting round the room draped in it. Then she slid out of the door and ran up the stairs to the flat roof, where she ripped off the black patch and found the gold Mother had hidden under it. She resewed it on after removing the money, and came down again and gave the cloak back to the pilgrim, offering him a night's lodging in addition. When she had seen him safely settled down she called to me:

'Thöpaga, your Master wants you.'

On my going into their room she gave me the seven pieces of gold and, in wonderment, I asked her how she had found them.

'Your mother's a shrewd woman, my boy,' she said. 'The valley facing north was the pilgrim's cloak, a valley that faces north never sees the sun neither can the sun's rays pierce that cloak. The cloud was naturally the black patch and the Pleiades she had embroidered on it; and her command to ask

39

information only of the pilgrim was to direct your attention to him.'

With our insoluble problem made to appear as simple as a child's game, we men were vastly impressed by this display of woman's wit and my Master said: 'Feminine intuition is proverbial; this is just another proof of it.' So I gave a small reward to the pilgrim, a larger one to my Teacher's wife and offered three of the gold pieces to my Teacher, with the request that he should instruct me in the art of making hailstorms and directing them; but he, in accordance with his pact, referred me back to my former Teacher for this, giving me a letter of recommendation and a scarf for him.

When I reached his house which I had only left a few weeks before, I gave him the letter and scarf and offered the remaining three pieces of gold, and after he had enquired about the success of my previous experiments in the Black Arts, he agreed to my request and promptly gave me the initiation. Then I was walled up in a cell for seven days while I practised my lesson. By the end of the week clouds gathered, thunder rumbled and the lightning flashed as I concentrated on my spells, but my Teacher would not let me launch the hailstorm until the time was right for the greatest destruction of crops, so I had to wait until the ears of barley were full and bending under their own weight. Then at last came the day when I was allowed to go to my own village to launch the great storm.

With me went a fellow pupil, one who was noted for his speed of running and outstanding strength, and the two of us disguised ourselves as pilgrims to escape recognition as we made our way in the direction of my home. On the road we could see fields on either side with abundant harvest; indeed the oldest inhabitants of the villages we passed through had never known such a crop in all their lives. All stood ready for reaping since, because of the size of the crop, a by-law had been passed that all should start harvesting together, that none should have an advantage.

What an arena for the display of my powers! We climbed one of the hills and looked down on the valley I had known from babyhood and there I lovingly set up the apparatus for launching my hailstorm. Then I began to chant the Spell.

Nothing happened! My heart stood still. Was I not to have my vengeance after all? I called upon the gods and poured out to them the tale of my sufferings and finally I struck the ground with my robe, weeping in my vexation and from the memories of the past.

At that a great black cloud gathered and soon the hail was crashing down, while the thunder roared and the lightning played all around us. In a short while the fields were a flattened misery, those beautiful fat ears of barley being strewn on the earth, and long ditches appeared on the hillsides as the hail coursed down them making river beds. Rain and a gale followed, and as we grew cold and wet we found a cave on the hill into which we went and made a fire from brushwood and sat and warmed and dried ourselves. While we sat there thawing out there came the sound of voices of some of the villagers who had been caught in the storm while out hunting, intending to bring home game for the harvest festival which all would have celebrated. This is what we heard:

'That fellow, Thöpaga, is the curse of the place. Heaven knows how many people he has killed. And now look at what he's done to our harvest—it's ruined! If only we could lay hands on him we'd tear him limb from limb.'

Just as they were passing the cave an elderly man said:

'Hush! Don't speak out loud. I can see smoke coming from that cave over there. We don't know who may be in it.'

And then a youngster said: 'I bet it's Thöpaga. He can't have seen us. Let's run down to the village and round up a posse to surround the cave; then we can take him and kill him before he does any more damage.'

We listened to their retreating footsteps and then my friend who was very fleet of foot and as strong as a lion, said:

'You get away quick and I will pretend I'm you and pull their legs.'

So we arranged to meet at the Tingri Inn. Knowing his powers as a runner I had no compunction about leaving him to it, but departed rapidly, having regretfully to forgo the pleasure of seeing my mother and sister when they were so near. A dog-bite delayed my arrival at the rendezvous on time, but when I found my companion I learned from him how he had fooled his pursuers, running some distance, then waiting for them and dashing off again. During his stops he would hurl taunts at them, shouting as if he were I: 'Look out! The first who attacks me will feel my next spell. I am gloating over all those I have killed already, and the harvest which I've destroyed—all my own work, too! If you don't let my mother and sister alone and treat them decently, I shall put a curse on the valley and blight it into a desert. You just see if I don't!' This so frightened his pursuers who thought he was myself that they held off and went into a huddle and finally decided that discretion was the better part of valour. They broke up therefore and went to their respective homes, each blaming the others for having raised my wrath.

He also told me that when he had reached Tingri Inn and inquired after me, the landlord had said that no one answering my description had been there. Then he had added: 'You pilgrims are always ready for a drink whenever there's any going. Well, there's a wedding in progress over yonder; why not join the guests? I can lend you a mug if you want.'

He accepted this kind offer and making his way to where the wedding breakfast was being held he found me there already and demanded to know what had held me up, so I told him about the dog-bite.

'Never mind,' he said and we went on, in due course arriving at the house of my former Teacher. To our astonishment we found that he already knew of the success of my spells, having learned it by the use of his magic. So he congratulated us before ever we had opened our mouths.

And this is how I came to dabble in the Black Arts and to do evil deeds by taking vengeance on my enemies, so that the deaths of many were to be laid at my door.

III

# The Search for Truth

We had listened intently so far to Milarepa's account of his troubles and the experiences of his childhood and to his excursions into the realm of Black Magic, and now we were eager to learn how he had made so great a switch from that to a deeply religious career. With such a beginning how could he have avoided sinking still lower? We were all wanting to know what happened next so I asked him: 'Sir, tell how it was you turned to religion and how did you get started on it?' Jetsun continued:

&#42;   &#42;   &#42;

As time went by reaction set in and I became filled with remorse for the deaths and damage I had caused, and I began to long for true Knowledge and a true Faith, until, at length, it became an obsession with me so that I could think of nothing else. Restlessness was an outstanding characteristic of this phase; if I sat down I wanted to be moving about, and if I was walking round I felt the urge to sit down, and I could neither eat nor sleep; yet somehow I could not bring myself to tell my Teacher about it and so continued serving him, ever looking for a suitable opportunity of asking his permission to leave him and take up a religious life.

Then one day, out of the blue, the chance was given to me. The Lama had been away for a few days to see an old friend of

44

his who was very ill and who died even while he was still with him; on his return, noticing his gloomy and preoccupied air, I ventured to ask him what was the matter, and this is the reply I received:

'Life is utterly impermanent. Last night my old friend passed away and I am deeply grieved about it. What misery there is in the world! My own life has been spent in the study and practice of Black Magic, and so I have added to the death and suffering already here. And you, too, my son, have followed in my footsteps and by now you have piled up quite a heap of bad *karma*, and this will be added also to mine for I am responsible for you. Would that I could now devote myself to the study of Truth. If you would stay and look after my children and pupils I would go—or else you go and learn and practise for us both the True Religion, and save me as well as yourself. You are young and energetic and have perseverance. Go and become a sincere Seeker.'

Nothing could have suited me better, for it was just what I had been wanting to hear him say; so I asked permission to set out at once, which he gave readily. In addition he made me a present of a yak and a bundle of woollen cloth and told me where to go, to Nar in the Tsang Valley, to a Lama who belonged to an ancient mystic sect and was reputed to have Higher Powers. To him, therefore, he would send me, and I was to study and practise hard. And so it was, one day, I came to Nar.

The Lama was away when I arrived, but I saw his wife and pupils and they told me where he was staying; I offered to pay anyone who would come with me as guide, and so at last I reached my destination and offered the yak and cloth as a present to the Lama. I told him what a wicked man I had been and how I had come from the Western Highlands at the request of my Teacher to search for Truth and earn for us both

45

deliverance from the round of births and deaths in this world of illusion. Then I begged him to give me instruction.

He accepted my gifts and said: 'My instruction is called that of The Great Perfection; being trebly perfect and doubly trebly perfect; perfect in the root, trunk and branches, that is, in the beginning, in the middle and in the end, and 'it blesseth him that gives and him that takes', its fruit being the knowledge of Yoga. Anyone meditating upon it for a single day only can be freed. To those spiritually as well as mentally developed, the mere hearing of it gives freedom without the need of meditation. It is for those most highly evolved. I shall give it to you.'

And then and there he initiated me and gave me the necessary instruction.

Inevitably in my wicked state this went to my head and I began to réflect on how the spells of Black Magic had taken one or two weeks to master and now I had found a Teaching which would deliver me overnight, whenever I chose to stop and think about it, and as the Lama had said highly evolved people could be delivered by the mere hearing of it, my head began to swell and I made no effort to meditate or practise what I had been taught.

A few days later, therefore, the Lama came to me and spoke some forthright words:

'Thöpaga,' he said, 'how right you were when you said you were a wicked man; perhaps, too, I boasted somewhat about the efficacy of my instruction. Anyway I see I cannot teach you or convert you; you are beyond my powers. In the Wheat Valley there lives a man who was a disciple of the great Indian saint, Naropa. He is known as Marpa the Translator, for he is a noted professor of texts. You and he have been associated before in previous lives. Go to him!'

Now at the name of Marpa the Translator a curious thrill

ran through my frame and my whole nervous system seemed
to be in a state of vibration, and thus I knew that he was my
true Guru. So, without wasting a moment I took my few
books, my only possessions now, and some food for the
journey, and set out, the question burning in my brain: When
shall I meet my Guru?

Later I learned that the night before my arrival Marpa had
had a strange dream, that his own Guru Naropa had come to
him with a dirty tarnished *dorje* symbol and a gold pot of holy
water and had told him that if he cleaned the symbol with the
water there would be great rejoicing in all the worlds. This
he did and he received much veneration from Beings in all
parts of the Universe in consequence. Now, oddly enough,
when his wife brought him his breakfast she also had a dream
to tell him of, similar in import, concerning the cleaning of a
reliquary.

Marpa did not confide his dream to her but merely told her
that he was going down to plough one of his fields and would
she see that a sufficient supply of beer was sent to him for
himself and some visitors he was expecting. Despite his wife's
protests that a Lama should not do the work for which he
paid common labourers, and what would the neighbours
think, he set out without troubling to argue the point, and
after doing a little ploughing sat down to refresh himself and
await my coming.

Meanwhile I was inquiring my way as I walked along the
road, asking passers-by where Marpa the Translator lived,
who was also known as The Great Yogi, but nobody seemed
to have heard of him. At last I found a man who had heard
of a Marpa, but did not recognise the rest of his high-sounding
title, so I asked him where Wheat Valley was and he pointed
out its direction and added that this was where Marpa lived.
I then asked if he was not known by any other name than

Marpa, and he said he was sometimes called Lama Marpa; from that I knew I was nearing the end of my journey and I continued on my way, asking every now and then for Marpa, but for a time without any further success.

Finally I met a young man, well groomed and expensively dressed, and I accosted him with my question, to which he replied:

'Oh, you must mean my father who used to sell everything there was in the house and then disappear into India for a while and return with rolls and rolls of papers. If it is him you will find him ploughing one of his fields to-day, which he's never done before.'

I could well imagine the first part of the description fitting Marpa the Great Translator but found it difficult to believe that he would have gone out ploughing, even if he *had* never done such a thing before. Still I wended my way to the field as directed.

. Even as my eyes fell upon the figure seated there my heart leapt and I felt again that same thrill that had run through me at the first sound of his name and I was filled with ecstasy. When once more in command of myself I asked him very respectfully where Marpa the Translator, the disciple of the famous Naropa of India, lived. He looked me up and down and then said: 'Where are you from and what do you want?'

I told him what I had told my previous Teacher, that I was a wicked man from the Western Highlands who had heard of the fame and knowledge of the Great Marpa and had come to learn Truth from him in order to obtain Deliverance.

The Lama replied: 'Very well, I will introduce you to him if you will finish ploughing this field for me.' And then, after offering me a refreshing drink of his beer, he left me to the ploughing, which together with the beer I finished quickly.

When a lad was sent to call me I went up to the house and

there found the Lama seated on a cushioned seat, having had a wash and change, but tell-tale marks of dirt still showed on his brow and nose. His well-rounded paunch now seemed to protrude even more than ever in front of him as he sat there. I looked round the room to make sure he was the same Lama and could see no other, and just then he spoke:

'Of course you did not know me. I am Marpa himself, so you may pay your respects.' At which I made profound obeisance, even touching his feet with my forehead, and then I repeated my self-accusation and begged for instruction and the wherewithal to live while receiving it.

He inquired about the nature of my misdeeds without showing any concern over them and when I offered myself, mind and body, he seemed to approve, but said that he could give me either instruction or my keep but not both; which did I want?

To this I said: 'I have come to you, Sir, for the Truth. I will get food and clothes where I can.'

And so I settled in. But when I was about to put my precious books on the altar shelf he stopped me, obviously sensing the nature of tomes on the Black Arts, and said: 'Take those away. I won't have my sacred volumes and holy reliques polluted by their presence.' So I kept them in my own little room and my Guru's wife proceeded to feed me and look after me well.

# IV

# Expiation

It now became necessary for me to raise the wherewithal by which I could make a gift to my Guru, so I set out on a begging expedition and after walking up and down the whole countryside I returned with many bushels of barley which had been given to me by various people. With half of the total I acquired a large and flawless copper vessel having four handles. Further bartering brought me some meat and beer. Stowing the remainder of the barley in a sack and with all my purchases piled into one bundle I went to my Guru's house.

It was a heavy load and when I arrived I dropped it off my back with a resounding clang onto the floor so that the whole house shook and my Master leaped to his feet and shouted: 'Oho, you think yourself very strong, don't you? Do you want to bring the house down about our ears by your display of strength? Take that sack away!' And with that he kicked my bushels of barley outside. I had to gather up my belongings and leave them on the path. What an irascible sort of man my Guru seemed to be! Yet my faith in him as Guru was unshaken, so I determined to behave with more decorum in his presence in future. Taking the things out of the copper vessel I brought the latter back into the house with some misgivings and, making a low obeisance, offered it to my Master.

He laid a hand upon it, thereby signifying his acceptance of it, to my great relief, and he seemed to become lost in prayer;

after a little while I saw the tears trickling down his cheeks, as he said, 'It is auspicious; I offer it to my Guru Naropa;' and raised his hands as if making an offering. Next he shook the handles of the urn and struck it violently until it resounded, and finally he took it to the altar and filled it with clarified butter which he kept to put in the altar lamps.

As the days passed into weeks I asked him time and again to give me instruction and at length he said: 'Many disciples of mine are waylaid and robbed as they try to come to me by the shepherd-bandits who infest the hills. Go and send a plague of hail upon their crops and then I will instruct you in the Truth.'

So off I went and launched a terrific hailstorm wherever I could find them, and returned to claim the promise, only to be met with a caustic refusal:

'What! You have the presumption to suggest that your little hailstones are adequate return for the Truth which I learned so hardly in India. If you are serious now, go and work a spell so that some other tribesmen in the Lhobrak region who have also robbed my disciples and even molested me will be destroyed. If you can prove yourself in this with a real piece of wizardry I will teach you the Truth by which Enlightenment and Buddhahood can be attained in a single lifetime.'

Again I obeyed him instantly; the effect of my magic was to make the tribesmen start fighting among themselves and many were killed as a result. Back I went, full of hopes that this time I might obtain my great desire, and once again my hopes were dashed. My Guru greeted me kindly enough and gave me the title of Great Sorcerer, but when I asked him for the Teaching he roared with laughter and asked how he could impart Truth in return for evil deeds, even if they had been well done. 'Go away,' he said, 'and first undo the damage you have just wrought; bring the dead back to life and restore the crops.' Then he began to rate me violently and I thought he was even going to beat me; in my despair I went away and wept and my Master's wife came and tried to comfort me.

Perhaps she spoke to her husband that night for next morning he found me and said:

'Perhaps I was a bit over-hasty last evening, but don't take it too much to heart. Be patient for I shall teach you in the end. Now, for the time being, as you seem to be a handy man, suppose you build a house for my son. When you have done that satisfactorily I will not only instruct you but also give you food and clothes during your period of study.'

'And what would happen if I should die before I have learned the Truth and secured Deliverance from my evil deeds?' I dared to ask, rather doubtfully.

'I assure you you will not die in the meanwhile,' he said with conviction. 'With my Teaching it is up to you, yourself, as you seem so full of energy, to win Enlightenment in one lifetime if you want it. My own sect differs a little from others in that we rely on emanations from Higher Sources and on direct intuition.'

Thus reassured I asked for plans of the house to be built and set to work with a will. On looking back now I can see that the Lama was really killing two birds with the one stone in what then happened. There as a particular site he wished to have a house on which other interested parties had agreed to keep open space, in which matter he had not been consulted, so that it was necessary to distract their attention from his true purpose by starting to build elsewhere; but he also wanted to try me to the uttermost in expiation of my evil deeds— and this indeed he was to do. In fact finally he achieved both ends.

The Lama began by taking me to a ridge of the mountain which faced east and ordered me to build there a circular house. It was half raised when he came along one day and said that he had changed his mind after further consideration, so I must demolish what I had done and carry the stones back to the place from which I had got them. Then he took me to another ridge which faced west and told me to build a crescent-shaped house; again the same thing happened. Once more I carried back the stones one by one, for he said he must have been a bit tight when he gave me such orders.

The third edifice was to face north and be triangular. Somewhat apprehensively I hinted that it was a waste of time and money to go on building and demolishing like this, but he replied that he was cold sober now and I was to carry out his wishes. Once again the rocks and stones were shouldered and the new building began to take shape.

Just as I feared! When it was half finished my Master came one day apparently in a very bad temper and demanded to know why I was constructing a house of that particular shape. Puzzled and despairing I reminded him that it was his own specification.

'I gave no such orders,' he bellowed at me, 'or if I did I must have been out of my mind at the time.'

'But, Sir,' I ventured to say, 'do you not remember me begging you to consider carefully before I started and you said you had done so and this was just what you wanted?'

'Oh, and what witness have you of that?' he sneered. 'Are you trying to destroy me with your spells that you want to put me into a house like a magical triangle? It's enough to drive all the evil spirits round here into a frenzy. Either demolish it and take those stones back again where you got them from or clear out altogether, for I shall not instruct you unless you do what I say.'

My Master seemed in a fury and I felt myself to be very hardly used, but since there was nothing else to do I humped each rock back to the quarry, despairing of ever being able to please him. Yet I needed the Teaching so much that I could do nothing else except obey him implicitly. By now I had a huge sore on my back between my shoulder-blades, but I dared not show it to him for fear he would be angry again, nor even to his wife lest she think I was trying to draw attention to all my hard work; so I carried on quietly, merely asking her to try and persuade her husband to give me some instruction.

The motherly old soul went to her husband then and told him outright that his useless building was wearing me out and she begged him to teach me a little.

'Go and cook a meal and invite him in,' said my Master, and this she promptly did and took me into dinner. After we had finished the Lama said:

'Great Sorcerer, don't accuse me, like you did yesterday, of things I haven't done. Now I will teach you something.' And with that he instructed me in the Three Refuges and Precepts and ended by saying: 'This is material Teaching. If you want Higher Knowledge to be imparted you must earn it.' Then he told me a story from the life of his own Guru Naropa and added: 'Of course this is far too high for you to attain to, I am afraid.' This touched my heart and brought tears to my eyes; I made a resolution to obey my Guru in everything.

A few days later he took me for a walk and when he had reached the site where he was banned from building he told me to construct an ordinary four-sided house there, nine storeys high; he promised faithfully that this would not be demolished and that when it was finished he would impart to me the Truth for which I longed.

Made wary by past experience I suggested tentatively that his wife might be made a witness of his words and I reminded him of what had happened with the former three houses:

54

## Expiation

'Last time you demanded that I produce a witness to the orders you had given me, Sir, and I hadn't one; so, please, this time, may your wife bear witness to them.'

This good lady, when she was told, said:

'Of course I will stand witness, but your Master is so dictatorial that he will take no notice of either of us. All this building is quite unnecessary and a sheer waste of time. Up and down, up and down, so it goes on. Besides he is not allowed to build on this site. But he'll never pay any attention to my weak voice and I shall only manage to rub him up the wrong way.'

At this Marpa said to his wife:

'Just do what you're asked to do and be a witness; otherwise mind your own business and I'll mind mine.'

With this amount of assurance I once again started laying foundations and building. One day three of the more advanced of the Guru's disciples thought for a joke to carry between them a huge boulder to the site. As it was of good size I made a cornerstone of it directly over the foundations and by the future door, and by the time my Master saw it I had reached the second storey.

'Where did you get this rock from?' he asked as he inspected my work.

'Three of your disciples brought it to me as a joke, Sir,' I replied.

'Then you had no right to use it. Take it out and return it to where they got it from,' he said.

I reminded him of his promise that his building should not be pulled down but he only remarked:

'I did not promise to let you use my chief disciples, who are Initiates, as builder's labourers. Besides you don't have to pull down the whole house, only remove the stone.'

But the whole wall on that side had to come down and I

55

laboriously manhandled the great rock back to its original bed. No sooner had I done that than the Lama said:

'Now you can bring it back yourself and reset it in the place you had it in before.'

It had taken three men to bring it the first time and now I alone had to put it into position, but somehow I managed to achieve it and the boulder remained a monument to my great strength.

Those people who had decided that building on this site should be prohibited now began to ask themselves whether Marpa was serious in his intentions to put up a house there. But his previous habit of ordering the destruction of my efforts misled them and so I had reached the seventh storey before they realised that at last this was to be a permanent house and not merely a spiritual and physical exercise for an erring novice. By then it was too late, Marpa had possession on his side and by the exercise of his Higher Powers those who had come with hostile intent ended by becoming his disciples. By this time I had a second sore on my back.

About this time the Lama was going to hold an Initiation Ceremony and his wife urged me to join with the candidates, thinking, as I did also, that all my labours and the nearly completed edifice would serve for the necessary gift to the Guru. Alas, for my hopes!

Seeing me seated at the end of the row Marpa said:

'Great Sorcerer, what offering have you brought with you?

'Sir,' I replied, 'you promised that when the house for your son was ready you would give me initiation and instruction, so I hope you will now grant me this favour.'

'You presumptuous young puppy,' the Master exclaimed. 'For a few stones and mud walls do you think I will give you the Higher Knowledge that I brought from India at such great cost to myself? Pay the Initiation fees or else get out of

56

*Expiation*

this sacred circle.' And he struck me and seized me by the hair and threw me out. Then, indeed, did I wish that I could die on the spot and I wept all night.

Mrs Marpa came to comfort me again and said:

'I can't understand my husband at all. He says he brought his Doctrine from India so as to help everybody with it and normally he will teach or preach to anyone who comes—even to the dog. Still, don't lose your faith in him.'

Next morning my Master said:

'Great Sorcerer, stop work on the house and start another one based on twelve pillars with a hall and shrine and when that is finished I will definitely give you the Teaching.' So once more I started and laid foundations and my good friend Mrs Marpa kept me supplied with food and beer and helped me with her advice and sympathy.

When this new edifice was nearly completed another disciple came for an Initiation of a still higher grade than the last. At once Mrs Marpa came along and said to me:

'We'll get you initiated this time for certain. Here, take this lump of butter and roll of blanket-cloth and copper vessel as your offerings and sit with the others.' I never thought to ask her where she had obtained the things and sat down quite hopefully.

'Great Sorcerer, where are your Initiation fees, as I see you sitting there with the candidates?' asked my Master.

I produced the butter, cloth and copper vessel which his wife had given me, but, alas, they were all things which had been brought as offerings by the other aspirants!

'What! You are offering me what is mine already, are you? How can you make a gift of them?' demanded the Lama. 'Either give me something of your own or out with you!' And with that he literally kicked me out of the room with many hard blows of his well-shod foot so that I felt like

57

sinking through the floor. Later I began speculating as to the reason for all this harsh treatment. Was I suffering *karma* for all my evil deeds in killing so many people and destroying such rich harvests with my hailstones? Or did my Master perceive that I was not yet fit to receive and practise the Doctrine? Or was it that he just didn't like me? Anyway, without religion life was not worth living and I began to contemplate committing suicide. At this point Mrs Marpa brought to me her share of the consecrated food from the ceremony in an effort to console me, but I had no appetite even for that and I cried far on into the night.

Next morning the Lama came to me and said: -

'Finish both the buildings then I will definitely give you Instruction.'

And so I went on building until yet another sore appeared on my back and pus and blood was running from all three so that my back was really nothing but one big sore. Now I had to show it to my good lady and reminded her of her husband's promises and asked her to use her influence with him to get me the Teaching. The sight of my back brought the tears to her eyes and she went at once to my Master and said:

'Great Sorcerer's body is in a terrible state from all this building; his legs and hands are cracked and bruised and his back has three large running sores. I have heard of saddle-sore donkeys and ponies before but never of a saddle-sore man. If people get to hear about it you will be disgraced—you, a highly respected Lama, will become known for your cruelty. Have a little feeling! And you did promise to give him the Instruction he is so longing for when he had finished the building.'

To which the Lama replied:

'Yes, indeed I did. I promised that when he had finished

the ten-storeyed house he should have it. Has he finished it?'

'But he has built a second place which is much bigger than the other,' argued Mrs Marpa with feeling.

'Much talk, little work, so runs the proverb,' retorted her husband. 'When he has finished the ten-storeyed house I will give him Instruction and not till then. But has he really got sores on his back?'

'If you weren't so tyrannical,' said his wife heatedly, 'you would have seen it for yourself. It is not that he has a sore on his back but that his back is just one big sore, as you should have noticed.' After rebuking him Mrs Marpa left quickly, but he only called after her:

'Let the boy come up here.'

Up I went hoping that at last my Master had relented and would teach me, but he merely told me to show him my back. On my doing so he examined it and said:

'Huh! Nothing to what my Guru, Lord Naropa, endured. He did not spare his body at all. I also have suffered quite considerably and laid down both my property and my body as a willing sacrifice in order to follow him. If you are truly a Seeker after Truth stop boasting about all you have done but plod on patiently till the building is finished.'

I leave you to imagine the depths of my feelings at these words!

Then he folded his robe into a pad and showed me how they pad saddle-sore horses and advised me to do the same.

'But what is the use of a pad to me when my whole back is an ulcer?' desperation drove me to ask.

'It will stop the dirt from getting in and making it worse,' he replied casually; 'you can still go on carrying stones and clay.'

If this was the command of my Guru I had to obey it, so I pressed on again carrying the loads in front of me now and so did the work. My Master noted it and privately he commended me in his heart, being moved to tears of happiness by my sincerity and faith in him. But my back sore grew worse until pain stopped me at last from working and once more I begged Mrs Marpa to plead with her husband to give me the Instruction or at least to allow me to rest awhile.

The Lamas's reply was: 'Teaching he cannot have until he has finished the building. He can rest, however, since this can't be helped. Anyway let him do what he can.' And then Mrs Marpa made me lie down and give my ulcers a chance to heal.

They were well on their way to being cured when my Master told me to get a move on and start work again. I was about to do so when his wife suggested to me a strategem for securing Instruction. I was to wrap up my few possessions in a bundle and take a bag of flour for provisions and set off down the road to a spot from which I could be both seen and heard from the house. She would then come running after me and pretend to be dissuading me from leaving and promise to try and get her husband to teach me.

And so it was: we two were arguing in the road when Marpa called out: 'What is this little drama that you two are acting?' and his wife called back: 'Great Sorcerer says he came a long way to take you as his Guru and to learn Truth from you. Instead all he has had is abuse and beatings. So now, in case he dies before obtaining the Truth he is going to leave you and look for another Guru. I am trying to stop him and have told him you will teach him in time.'

'Is that so?' said Mr Marpa, and coming down from the house he proceeded to cuff me soundly, saying: 'When you came you offered yourself to me, body, speech and mind. You belong to me, so where do you think you are off to now? I have the right to cut you up into a hundred little

pieces and no one could stop me. And what's this?'—the bag
of flour had fallen down and burst under his assault—'What
right have you to take food from my house?' He then knocked
me down and gave me a violent beating, after which he walked
back to the house with the damaged bag of flour.

My grief now knew no bounds. I was also overawed by
the imperiousness of his behaviour and told myself this was
the result of conspiring with his wife behind his back. So I
retired to my bed to weep and to recover from the effects of
the beating. Mrs Marpa, as usual, came to comfort me and
said it was obvious that neither persuasion nor strategem
would move the Lama but she assured me he would teach
me in the end. Then she added:

'Meanwhile I will teach you something,' and she proceeded
to instruct me in a system of meditation which did something
to satisfy my thirst for knowledge; I was very grateful to her
for what she told me, although, of course, she could not give
me the complete instruction. To show my gratitude, therefore, I went out of my way to do little things for her and made
her a milking stool and another for when she was roasting
barley in the front yard.

But by now I was seriously considering going to look for
another Guru, yet I knew that my present one was the only
Guru with the Doctrine of Deliverance from the Wheel of
Rebirth. This was what I particularly wanted as I knew that
if I did not obtain it my evil deeds would drag me down
after my death to a terrible fate. So I decided to take Naropa
as my example in courage and fortitude and secure my deliverance by dogged determination. And in this frame of mind
I continued building and carting stones and mud.

Then came a time when yet another Initiation ceremony
was to be performed, the candidate, one Ngodun, bringing
with him priceless gifts and a large entourage. Once again

Mrs Marpa came to me urging me to take my seat with the others and giving me a turquoise of her own as my fee should the Lama demand any—which, of course, he did.

I presented the turquoise.

'Great Sorcerer, where did you get this from?' he asked.

'Your good wife gave it to me, Sir,' I replied.

'Call Damema here.' And I went to find her.

'Damema,' he said, when she had come, 'how did we get this turquoise?'

Although apprehensive and very respectful, Mrs Marpa was not going to overlook the 'we'.

'My husband,' she said, 'this turquoise is not ours, it is mine; it was given me before my marriage by my parents. They knew of your irascibility and for fear that our marriage might not last they gave me this as a safeguard should I ever want to leave you. But knowing how this lad here is so desperate for Teaching, I gave it to him. He has worked so hard and been so patient; so do, please, accept the turquoise from him and give him the Initiation. And you, Ngogdun and the rest, add your pleas to mine on his behalf.'

But the rest of the candidates had not her courage and dared not speak, contenting themselves with rising and making an obeisance in the direction of the Guru with the one word: 'Please!'

Marpa then said to his wife: 'What a silly woman you are, Damema, your stupidity nearly lost me this turquoise. When you, yourself, belong to me, all you have, including this turquoise, is obviously mine also. Great Sorcerer, if you have anything of your own to give, bring it along and I will give you the Initiation; but this belongs already to me.'

Naturally I had nothing of my own, but I lingered on in the hopes that he might relent. However, I only succeeded in rousing his temper, for he suddenly leapt up with the same

abuse that I had heard before and struck me a blow on the
head that knocked me down; then he picked me up bodily
and threw me on to my back and finally he seized a stick to
beat me. But Ngogdun, the principal candidate, intervened
and held him back by force, while I, in sheer terror, jumped
through the window; this secretly frightened him. I landed
unhurt in body, but deeply wounded in spirit and this time
really resolved on suicide. As usual my comforter came with
her sympathy to console me and said:

'Great Sorcerer, don't be so upset. You are the dearest and
most faithful pupil ever. If you really want to go and look
for another Guru I will give you money and presents for him.'
The good soul stayed with me all night and we cried together,
and she even missed the evening *puja* with her husband.

Next morning my Master sent for me. Was it, at last, to be
for instruction? But no! He merely asked me if my faith in
him had been shaken or my affection turned to dislike?

'No, Sir,' I replied, 'for it is only my own evil deeds of the
past that are preventing my Initiation and I am filled with
remorse for them,' and I burst into tears.

'What's this?' he exclaimed. 'By crying thus you accuse me.'
And he again became angry.

I left the room precipitately, feeling as if my heart would
break and in bewilderment. How I wished I had but one
half of the wealth with which I had left home. I should get
nothing from this Guru without a handsome present—nor
from any other Guru for that matter, for such is the custom.
Having nothing I would be likely to die in the bondage of my
sins—so why go on living any longer? Or what else to do?
Think, think, of something. Should I go into service and save
up wages and tips and then return? Or go back home to
Mother? That would be risky with the villagers in such a rage
at me. Still, I had to go and look for money somehow or

find the Teaching elsewhere. Yes. Go, go . . . the words kept hammering at my brain.

I collected my books together but this time took no provender from the house, nor did I confide in Mrs Marpa. But after I had gone four or five miles I began longing to see her again to thank her for her kindness, and my own ingratitude at having left her without even saying 'Thank you' filled me with regret. At noon I begged some barley meal and borrowed utensils and cooked myself a frugal lunch, all with considerable difficulty, and began reflecting that having my keep for so long must have represented at least half of my wages, and that it had never involved the trouble the preparation of this meal had been. I was in half a mind to go back but could not quite bring myself to do so.

Then, when I was going to return the utensils I had borrowed, an old man stopped me and said:

'Tut, tut! What is a young man like you, well able to work, doing begging? Why not earn your bread and butter by reading the Scriptures, if you can read; or, if you can't, why not get a job of some sort? Can you read, by the way?'

I told him I could and that I was not a professional beggar.

'All right,' he said, 'come home with me and read the Scriptures to me and I will pay you well.'

I gladly accepted the offer and began reading to him the *Book of Transcendental Wisdom* and in due course I came on to the story of the Saint, who, being penniless, had sold his own flesh for the Doctrine. Indeed he would have sold his own heart if need be. And by comparison my trials began to dwindle into nothingness. Then once again I started hoping that perhaps the Lama would relent and give me the Teaching after all. And anyway, I told myself, Mrs Marpa had promised to help me find another Guru. So I returned the way I had come.

# Expiation

Later I learned that while I had been away Mrs Marpa, as soon as she had realized that I had gone, went to her husband and said:

'Well, are you satisfied now? Your deadly foe has left you!'

'What do you mean?' he asked quickly.

'Poor Great Sorcerer, of course. Didn't you treat him as if he were your worst enemy?'

At this the Lama was obviously deeply disturbed and uttered a prayer for the return of his destined pupil; then he wrapped his head up in a mantle and sank into profound silence.

When I got back and paid my respects to my Guru's wife she was overjoyed to see me again.

'It's the best thing you could have done,' she said, 'I think at last your Master will give you some Teaching; for when I told him you had gone he even shed some tears and prayed aloud that his gifted and destined pupil might be restored to him. I think it was he who influenced you from a distance to return.'

Privately I felt that she was merely saying this to put new life into me, for how did his refusal to teach me anything add up with a prayer for my return? If he had really called me 'gifted' then that was something to congratulate oneself on. But I was very apprehensive of his not only refusing to teach me himself but also of his preventing me from finding another Guru.

Mrs Marpa now went to her husband and said: 'Great Sorcerer couldn't bring himself to leave us after all. He has come back. May I tell him to come in and make his obeisance to you?'

'It's not for love of us he has returned,' said Marpa caustically, 'but he may come in and make his proper salutation.'

So in I went and knelt before him and my Master said: 'Great Sorcerer, don't be such a shilly-shally. If you are really determined to obtain the Teaching you must be prepared to sacrifice even your life itself. Now go. Finish the last three storeys of the house and then your great desire will be fulfilled. But if you have any doubts, go, for I am only wasting good food on you!'

Not daring to speak I departed, but outside I said to Mrs Marpa: 'Madam, I want very badly to see my mother again and I am quite convinced the Lama will not give me the Teaching. If I were sure he would I would willingly stop and complete the building, but he only makes one excuse after another. I know I will not get it even if I do finish the house; so please let me go home.' I made her a low bow and was on the point of leaving when she said:

'You are quite right. I did promise to find you another Guru, and there is a pupil of the Lama's who has all his Teachings, Ngogdun-Chudor—the one who came here for the last Initiation Ceremony. If you stay for a few days and pretend to work I will find some way of helping you get what you want from him.' Very pleased with this arrangement I went to work with a will.

During his lifetime, the Master Naropa used to keep the tenth of each month as a special holy day and Marpa had continued the practice. It was for this day that his wife now devised a scheme to deceive my Guru. Brewing the usual beer extra strong, she divided it into three vessels, and from the first which was the most potent she plied her husband with drink; the disciples were served from the next strongest, while she and I merely sipped from the third jar. Soon the household were all fast asleep. Then she stole into Marpa's room and removed certain of his things, including two relics of Naropa, his rosary and garland. These she gave to me wrapped up in a presentation scarf, with a letter she had forged in which Marpa asked Ngogdun to give me the Initiation and Teaching, and she told me where to find him. And so with rising hopes I set out towards the Central Province of Tibet.

Two days later the Lama asked his wife what I was doing.

'I expect he's somewhere on the road, but I can't tell you exactly where,' she replied as casually as she could.

'Where has he gone and when?' demanded her husband.

'He was saying that however much work he did for you he could never please you, and you gave him no Teaching but only beatings and scoldings instead, so he was going to look for another Guru. As you would probably have beaten me, too, if I had come to tell you, I thought it better not to. There was no holding him.'

The Lama's face turned black with rage.

'When did he leave?' he thundered.

'Two days ago,' said his wife. This was received in silence, then, after a while, he said as if to himself:

'My pupil can't have gone very far by now.'

Actually I had just reached Ngogdun's residence about that time. He was by now a High Lama and I found him engaged on a philosophical lecture to his disciples. I can still recall the words of the text he was reading: 'I am the Expounder. I am the Hearer. I am the Teacher of the world and I am the Devotee. I am the Being who has passed beyond all states of worldly existence and I am the Blissful One.' At this point he caught sight of me on the outskirts of the group and I made obeisance to him while still at some distance. He acknowledged it by taking off his hat to me.

From the type of obeisance I used he knew that I was one of Marpa's pupils and my arrival, coinciding with that particular stanza he had been reciting, seemed to be a good omen; indeed, he prophesied on the strength of it that I should one day become a Master of Religious Knowledge. Then he sent one of his disciples over to me to ask who I was and what was my business.

I replied without much regard to the truth that Marpa was too busy to teach me so he had sent me there, and that I had brought with me certain relics of Naropa as a present for the Lama. He then realised I was Great Sorcerer and the relics filled him with such delight that he promptly ordered a special ceremonial for their reception.

When I came to where he was waiting I again prostrated myself and offered the packet. He took it, deeply moved, placed the relics on the altar and then read aloud Mrs Marpa's letter which ran thus:

'I am about to go into close retreat and as Great Sorcerer is eager to obtain Instruction I am sending him to you for Initiation and Consecration. Please give him this and the Teaching on my authority. In token I send you Naropa's rosary and garlands.'

When Ngogdun had finished reading the letter he said that he would certainly give me the Initiation and Consecration, at which my heart leapt, but with his next words my hopes sank again.

'I have a number of pupils who are waylaid and robbed as they come to me at a place called Dol. Please go and launch a hailstorm against the shepherd bandits of the place and teach them a lesson; then when you have done it I will give you the Initiation and Consecration.'

How I cursed the day I ever took up Black Magic and learned the power of making hailstorms. I seemed unable to escape from my past. Here I had come in search of Truth and again was being asked to add to my evil deeds. Why had I acquired this regrettable ability for taking life and injuring people and property? Still, there was no help for it; if I did not obey him he would not give me the Teaching. So I left

68

immediately and took lodging with an old woman in the village where my devastation was to take place. But as the clouds gathered and the first great drops fell, the old woman, who was my landlady, burst into tears and lamentations, crying out that she would starve to death if her crops were ruined.

This upset me so much, for she was a pitiable old thing, that at considerable risk to myself, I got her to make a rough diagram of her field. It was triangular with a prolonged tail-piece and I swiftly covered it with a frying-pan, then concentrated my thoughts on her field being undamaged. The result was that the whole was unscathed except the tail which stuck out beyond the frying-pan. When all was over I went out to survey the desolation. The old woman's field showed fresh and green, with the exception of the tail which matched the devastated countryside around.

On my way back to Ngogdun again I met a shepherd and his child who had lost their flocks in the deluge and I made sure they spread it around that the storm was the result of their molesting innocent pilgrims and that in future the practice should cease. They were then so overawed by Ngogdun's powers that they all became his devotees.

As I walked along I saw a bunch of dead birds under a hedgerow where they had sought shelter and dead rats and other birds, and I was filled with the enormity of my actions. Collecting all the dead birds and animals I filled my hat and cloak with them and when I reached Ngogdun's house emptied them out on the floor in front of him.

'Master,' I said, 'I came here to find the true Teaching and have merely added to my sins. Have pity on me for I am so wicked.' And with this I burst into tears.

But the Lama said: 'Don't despair. There's no need for all this fear. Just trust in me and no harm will come to the birds and beasts that have been killed through your storm. If you don't believe me, watch!' For a few minutes he sat silent with eyes shut, then suddenly snapped his fingers and lo! the dead birds rose up and flew away and the rats scampered off into the nearest holes! I could see that the Lama had reached Buddhahood and I was profoundly moved with admiration and gratitude.

And so at long last I received the Initiation which Ngogdun himself had received at the hands of Marpa. Then I found a cave facing his house and, cleaning it out and making it habitable, I then walled myself up in it, leaving only a small aperture for food and water to be passed through, in the manner traditional. My Guru had explained to me the method of meditation and this I practised; but despite every effort I made no spiritual progress, for I had not Marpa's consent.

One day Ngogdun came to my cave and asked if I had had a certain type of experience during my meditation. I had to admit that I had not.

'How's that?' he asked. 'This particular practice never fails to produce spiritual development unless there is a block somewhere. What can it be? It cannot be that our Head Guru did not give his permission, for we have the letter and relics to prove it. Any way carry on and let us see.'

This alarmed me so much I nearly blurted out the truth, but courage failed me; however, it brought home to me as nothing else the need for making my peace with Marpa. Meanwhile I went on practising the meditation as best I could.

Soon after this Lama Marpa, who had in the meantime found someone else to finish his son's house, wrote to Ngogdun-Chudor and asked him to send a number of loads of twigs to fringe the thatching; he added that when the ornamentation was finished Lama Ngogdun was to come himself for the consecration ceremony, at which he intended also celebrating his son's coming of age. In the letter he added that if that young blackguard Thöpaga were with him would he bring him back at the same time.

The Guru came to my cave and read the letter out to me through the aperture, saying: 'It looks from this as if you didn't have your Master's permission to receive the Initiation.'

'No, Sir,' I admitted, 'the Lama himself did not give me permission; it was his wife who wrote that letter and gave me the relics.'

'H'm,' he grunted, 'so that is why you have had none of the usual experiences and it has all been a waste of time. You should have known you could not make proper use of an Initiation if you had not received your Guru's permission for it. Anyway, he says I am to bring you back with me. Do you want to go or not?'

I did, and I begged him to let me go as his attendant, so he said that when he knew the correct date for the ceremony he would let me know. Till then I was to continue in my hermitage.

When his porters returned after delivering the branches and told him the date he came again to me, and we had a long talk through the aperture about the approaching festival. At one point I found an opportunity of asking whether any reference had been made to me.

'Yes,' said Ngogdun, 'Mrs Marpa asked after you and what you were doing and she was told that you were in retreat and preferred your own company; she said it was due to your having left this die behind and she asked one of the porters to tuck it securely in his loincloth and to give it to you.' He then passed the die through the aperture to me.

When he was gone I was moved to play with it and threw it several times, but then it occurred to me that I had never shown any desire for dice games in Mrs Marpa's presence and I began to wonder why she had sent it at all, especially as it was that very thing which had ruined the family fortunes of my ancestor. Was it a token of her contempt for me? The thought was unbearable and in sudden rage I hurled it to the floor, at which it split open and a small piece of paper fell out. Picking this up I read:

'Son, your Guru is now disposed to give you the Teaching and Initiation you want. So come back with Lama Ngogdun.'

Now I danced with joy, up and down my little cave.

Then came Ngogdun and said: 'Great Sorcerer, get ready for the journey.' I did speedily. The Lama himself made a collection of all his movable property, other than what he had been given at any time by Marpa, to take with him as a gift for Guru. And a wonderful collection it was, too: books, relics, jewels, gold, plate vessels, livestock and so on. Only one item he omitted, a lame old she-goat which could not have kept up with the flocks and herds. To me he gave a silk scarf as my offering, his wife adding also a bag of grated cheese as a present for Mrs Marpa.

We set out with a large retinue. When we were still some way from our destination Ngogdun told me to go on ahead and inform his Guru of our coming and to ask for a little beer to be sent out to us for refreshment. And so I came back to my Master's house. Meeting his wife first, I gave her the bag of cheese and paid my respects. Then I told her Ngogdun was on his way and asked if she would send some refreshments out to him. She was very pleased and told me to go into the house and pay my respects to my Master.

I found him meditating in an upper room. I made my obeisance and tried to present the scarf, but he turned his back on me. Going round to the other side of him I did it again

72

and this time he made a half-turn away from me, so, plucking
up my courage, I spoke out:

'Respected Guru, although you are angry with me and
refuse to accept my obeisance, I have come to tell you that
Lama Ngogdun is on his way here with all his possessions,
as a gift for you'—and here I ran over a list of the property
he had brought—'so should he not be well received? If you
please, be kind enough to send some beer and refreshments
to him while he is still on the road.'

Apparently in a fury the irascible Lama burst out into abuse
once again:

'What reception did I ever get after plodding my weary
way back from India with such a precious burden as the
Teachings on my shoulders? Did even a lame bird come out
to chirrup a greeting at me? Am I, Marpa the Translator,
to go and receive Ngogdun just because he brings me a few
straggly cattle? Never! If that's what he expects he had
better turn round and go back the way he came.'

I left hurriedly and told Mrs Marpa, who said, 'Your Guru
is indeed an irritable man. Ngogdun is a great man and
should be properly received. Come on! Let's go together and
meet him.'

'Oh no!' I cut in, shocked, 'he doesn't expect *you* to go.
Just give me a little beer and I will take it back to him.'

But she would have none of it; instead she ordered some
of the disciples to bring a good supply of brew and we went
out together to receive Ngogdun.

A grand party had been arranged for this day to celebrate
not only the consecration of the house but also the coming
of age of Marpa's son; there were many guests present and a
big feast had been prepared. Marpa, when all was ready,
sang a benediction upon the company, invoking a blessing on
his Sect, the Teaching, himself and his disciples, on all good

thoughts and actions and finally on the assembled gathering of Lamas and laymen.

When he had finished Ngogdun came forward and offered his gifts making at the same time the following speech:

'Most Reverend Master; it goes without saying that I and all I have is yours. Herewith I offer to you all that is here. The only thing I have left behind is a lame old she-goat which could not have kept up with the rest. In return for this offering I beg you to confer on me the Precious Initiation and the deeper Esoteric Truths which are for oral transmission only, together with the necessary books.' He then made a prostration to a well-pleased Marpa who replied:

"H'm! If this is so I can tell you I have some of the rarest and most potent truths and Scriptures. They belong to a Path by which it is possible to obtain Nirvana in this very lifetime instead of having to be reborn again and again through countless ages. But the giving of such Truths have very strict conditions attached to them. Unless, therefore, you go home and bring back the lame old goat you left behind I am afraid I shall not be able to confer them upon you. And all the others you have already.'

On confirming that if he himself fetched the goat Marpa would give him the Initiation he wanted, Ngogdun set off home again the following morning and in a few days returned with the goat on his shoulder. At such devotion the old Guru was deeply moved and said:

'A devoted and faithful seeker after Truth should indeed be like you. I have little use for a lame old she-goat but I wanted to emphasise the importance and value of the Truths.' And shortly afterwards he gave Ngogdun the Initiation he was seeking.

The feasting continued over a period of time, different guests being present on different days, and one day when there

were only some of his disciples who had come from afar,
together with members of his own family, Marpa suddenly
fixed his eye on Ngogdun and pointed his finger at him, saying
accusingly:

'Ngogdun-Chudor, what is your excuse for having given
an Initiation to this disreputable blackguard, Thöpaga?' And
he looked meaningly at the stout stick he held in his hand.

The poor High Lama was terrified and stammered out:

'Dearest Master, you yourself commanded me in a letter
you had signed and sealed to initiate Thöpaga, and you sent
Naropa's garlands and rosary as a token. I haven't done
anything wrong so please don't be angry with me.' And he
looked round uneasily perhaps for a line of retreat.

It was my turn next. The accusing finger moved to my
direction:

'Where did you get them from?' demanded its owner
menacingly. Panic gripped me, my heart started to thump
and my knees felt weak. Trembling all over I stammered out
that I had received them from his lady wife.

Marpa immediately jumped up from his couch and made
towards his wife, stick in hand and with obvious intent to
administer punishment, but his wife, well able to take care of
herself through long experience, had taken a seat near the
door. She slipped neatly out and ran to the chapel where she
bolted herself in. Marpa thundered on the door but was unable to open it and so returned to his other victim.

Marpa sat down again and said: 'Ngogdun-Chudor, for
having done what I did not tell you to do, I command you to
go home and bring back that rosary and the garlands of
Naropa immediately.' Then he covered his head and sat in
silence and no one disturbed him.

Ngogdun bowed and departed in silence and as he came
out I stopped him, for I had made my escape at the same time

as Mrs Marpa and had hidden, and now I begged him with tears to take me with him. But he was fearful and said:

'If I take you again without your Guru's express command there will only be another painful scene. Stay for the present. If our Guru will do nothing but ill-treat you I will do whatever I can to help you.'

'It's all the fault of my own wicked past that I am in trouble and now I have got you and Mrs Marpa involved in it too. I have given up hope of getting the Teaching. I might as well cut short my life.' And, indeed, I turned away intending to commit suicide then and there.

But Lama Ngogdun said: 'Don't do that, Brave Great Sorcerer! According to the Teaching our bodily principles and faculties are divine. If we cut short our lives voluntarily we incur the guilt of killing the divine in ourselves and for this we should be duly punished. There is no greater sin than suicide. Even in the Scriptures it is condemned roundly. For goodness sake understand and get the idea out of your head! After all our Guru may yet give you the Teachings, and even if he will not there is always someone else who will.'

And so he tried to comfort me. Some of the other disciples also came along and sympathised, trying to console me. But my heart felt as if it would break, my suffering was so intense.

So now you know, Rechung and my other pupils, just how much I had to endure at the start of my search for Truth as the result of my own evil past.

*        *        *

We had scarcely been able to restrain our tears at his graphic account; indeed, one or two had all but fainted with emotion.

# V

## Initiation

Once more it fell to my lot to prompt our beloved Guru to tell us how he met with success at last and why Marpa changed in his attitude towards him.  And so Milarepa continued:

★        ★        ★

Well, all the pupils were in a great state because of our Master's violent temper, but after a while his mood changed and became, for him, quite sunny. He called for his wife to come to him, and while one of the disciples went for her he asked:

'Where are Ngogdun-Chudor and the other pupils?'

'Master,' one replied, more daring than the rest, 'you commanded Ngogdun to go home and fetch Naropa's relics; as he started he saw Great Sorcerer in much distress and he is still trying to console him.' Marpa asked for further details and when he had received them his eyes filled with tears and he spoke half to himself:

'Thus must it be for disciples of Truth; He has become just what I wanted him to become. Call my pupils for I feel sorry for them all.'

Then one of them went to look for Ngogdun and told him what Marpa had said and how his temper seemed to have evaporated and that he was quite kindly disposed and wanted him to come. At which I complained enviously of the others' favours and wept that our Master could be so feeling towards them and so harsh always to myself; and Lama Ngogdun stayed with me to comfort me.

'He never wants to see me,' I sobbed, 'or if he does it is only to scold or beat me. Ngogdun sent one of the pupils to ask Marpa whether his amnesty included myself or not, adding that if something was not done about it he would not be responsible for what I might do to myself, such distress was I in.

And when told Marpa made the astonishing reply: 'Formerly Great Sorcerer's point would have been right, but not today. Today he is to be the chief guest. Damema, go and invite him yourself.'

Along came Mrs Marpa, her kindly old face wreathed in smiles and she said to me:

'Great Sorcerer, I think you have found favour with your Guru at long last. He has just told me to call you and said that you were to be the chief guest. He seems to have done a complete turn about. Come along now; we'll go in together.'

Not wholly convinced that such good fortune could be mine after so many previous disappointments, I followed her very diffidently and sat down. Then Marpa began to make quite a speech.

'Having thought it over I don't think anyone is really to blame. To make Great Sorcerer expiate his sins I made him do all that building single-handed. Had it been a mere selfish aim of mine, I could have got more out of him if I had been kind and coaxed him, but my temper was purposeful, so don't blame me. As for my wife here, all her maternal instincts were raised at the harsh treatment I gave to Great Sorcerer who was so willing and patient, so one can hardly blame her for forging the letter and stealing the tokens, serious though the offence was. As for Great Sorcerer, himself, he was quite

78

right to go to any lengths to obtain the Teaching. Ngogdun, you of course could not have known and so are free of blame, as you yourself said. And I knew nothing at the time of the forged letter or the Initiation that had been conferred, otherwise I could have tried Great Sorcerer to the bitter end. My failure here was what made me angry. It was not, of course, ordinary bad temper, but a religious anger which is different, solely for the purpose of eliciting repentance in the delinquent, so if any of you here have been shocked at my outbursts do not lose faith in me; I knew just what I was doing. Had I been able to plunge him into the depths of despair nine times he would have been wholly cleansed and would not have been reborn again, but would have attained Nirvana. As it is there is still a little demerit left he has to work off, thanks to the well-meaning if misguided Damema and her soft heart. However, he has been cleansed eight times and has had many minor chastenings as well for lesser misdeeds. Now I will give him the Initiation and the Teaching and will maintain him while he is in retreat in a sealed hermitage.'

I had to pinch myself to make sure that I was awake and that it was not all a dream; tears of sheer joy came as I made obeisance at my Master's feet. Damema and Ngogdun and the rest did not know what to admire most in our Guru, his sternness and inflexibility in respect of me, his mercy and kindness eventually, or his wisdom and insight. They recognised that he had reached Buddhahood himself and with renewed faith and still deeper affection they bowed down before him expressing their delight and gratitude at the turn of the tide. All was smiles and laughter as we ate the sacred cakes, a happy gathering.

That same night offerings were laid on the altar and my head was shaved and I was dressed in a monk's robe, being ordained a novice and taking the Bodhisattva vow.'

As Lama Marpa blessed the sacred wine in the skull-cap, everyone saw a rainbow emitted from it. He poured out some in libation to his tutelary Deities, then drank from the skull and handed it to me to finish, which I did. He promised to give me the Complete Initiation the following day.

He expounded some of the Higher Teaching with the aid of diagrams and gave me permission to read the Tantras; then followed this up with an explanation of certain methods of meditation. Finally he laid his hand on my head and said:

'My son, I knew from the start you were a true Seeker.' And he told me about the dreams he and his wife had had the night before I arrived. 'That is why I went out pretending to plough my field, but in reality to meet you,' he went on. 'Your finishing the beer and the ploughing was a sign that you would be a worthy pupil who would drink of the Truth that I would offer you.' He then explained the significance of the copper vessel that I had bought for him. Indeed, it seemed as if he had done nothing at all without a purpose, and that purpose was my welfare. 'And now,' he ended, 'as you bore everything with so much patience and meekness and without losing your faith in me, you, too, shall have disciples of like energy, faith and intelligence who will be a credit to you as you have been to me.'

Thus it was that my Guru encouraged, praised, and gladdened me, and that my happy days began.

# VI

# The Guru's Teaching

I asked Milarepa then: 'Master, did you go off straight away into the wilderness to meditate alone on the Truths you had received?' Milarepa continued:

*    *    *

My Guru told me to settle in a rock cave which he stocked with provisions for me and periodically he came to pass food through the aperture. There I sat on my cushion for eleven months meditating with my body rigid, a butter lamp perched on my head; while it remained alight I would continue in my meditation and only rested when it went out, were it night or day. Then, after eleven months had passed, my Master and his wife came to me and said I had done well but now I was to come out of my retreat and join them in a feast and then recount to him the results of my meditation. This I was most reluctant to do but because my Guru had ordered it I had to obey; I did not hasten to complete the task of pulling down the wall but was trying to delay. Then Mrs Marpa came and asked: 'Son, aren't you coming?'

'I don't feel like pulling down the wall,' I replied.

'Never mind that,' she said. 'You know the Omens are very important and they have indicated that you should come out. Besides, your Master's temper is not too good and if your delay caused any bad omens to appear I should not like

81

to be in your shoes. Come on, I'll help you pull it down.'
With that we went at it together and soon I saw the light of
day again. I went out into the world feeling quite lost.

'While we two, who are father and son, shall discuss
Meditation,' said Lama Marpa, 'you, Damema, go and cook
up a fine dinner.'

During the meal he asked me what experiences I had had
during my retreat and what insight I had gained. 'Take your
time and tell me,' he said. So, never having lost the art of
bursting into song extempore, I began by making a hymn of
praise to my Guru and his wife in worship to him who had
done so much for me, and when I had finished I told him of
the Truth that I had perceived in the course of my meditations.

'Most Supreme Master, who are the Buddha, Vajra-Dhara,
himself, to whom my debt is infinite and beyond all measuring, I have perceived a little of the Truth as a return for all
that you have done for me. And this is what I have understood, if you will be kind enough to listen patiently to me:

'The system of the twelve *nidanas* I have grasped, which
show the interdependence of everything in this world upon
everything else, and that in this manner my body and presence
in life here is due to Ignorance, for Ignorance is the prime
cause of rebirth. To those who can realise this, their very
bodies may be the means of their deliverance from rebirth;
but to the rest—their bodies are but the fetters that bind them
to the Wheel of Life and Death. Hence our life is the dividing
life between the higher or the lower, according as to whether
we progress upward or fall further downward. Each must
decide for himself which way he goes, hence the opportunity
he has as the result of having been born a man is one not to
be lightly thrown away, for the effects of our choice are far-reaching. In holding to you, my Guru, I hope to pass over
from this ceaseless round of existence, the source of all pain

and suffering; but in order to achieve this I needs must take
Refuge in the Triple Gem, the Buddha, the Dharma and the
Sangha, and to follow the Precepts. In this too the Guru is
the chief means to success and happiness. Hence I am aware
of the need of implicit obedience to my Guru's commands
and of keeping my faith in him utterly and unimpaired.

'This was the first step in my Understanding. The next
followed from it. I meditated deeply on the rareness of birth
as a well-endowed human being amidst all the possible forms
of life there are, on the uncertainty that shrouds the moment
of death, on the inevitable effect of one's actions, on the
ubiquity of suffering in the world; all of which things must
surely make one desire to be free of such existence once and
for all. But to obtain such freedom one must follow the
Noble Eightfold Path, the only means to Emancipation. And
from this Path one must go on up to Higher Paths, never for
a moment ceasing to work upon oneself and observe the Precepts, performing them and renewing one's vows as necessary. He who seeks only his own freedom and happiness takes
the Lower Path, but he who feels Love and Compassion to
other Beings so that he wants to help them towards Emancipation, too, he has set foot on the Higher Road, and to leave
the Lower Path and to take to the Higher means one must
know exactly whither one is going and what is the goal.

'The third step I made was to realise that a Guru was necessary for such an endeavour, a Guru who is himself highly
developed and knowledgeable, who is Master of the methods
of Initiation and who knows what is best suited for his *chela*,
for he alone can explain the Final Goal to him. The ceremony
of Initiation gives a power to the mind for mastery of deep
Truth and, in meditating on the Final Goal one must make
every effort, using academic knowledge of grammar and
logic as well as mental and moral reasoning and the practice

of self-observation to discover the Truth that "There is no such thing as I" and how all our reasoning and learning based on this assumption of an "I" is fallacious.

'By dint of hard work and much practice one may come to a stage when one's mind is perfectly at rest, where all mental motion ceases and then time itself may seem to stand still. When one has reached this stage then can one exert the faculty of consciousness to gain a state of ecstasy—the ecstasy of a quiescent consciousness. Ordinary individuals who think in terms of "I" and "the rest" can never experience it, but one must be well on the Path to Buddhahood to win to it and so by controlled Thought and concentration on visualisations one treads the Path, the visualisations of deities being merely signs upon the Way and of no intrinsic value of their own.

'So, in effect, what is needed is mental quiescence, unbounded energy, a keen analytic sense, and a clear and inquiring mind; these are like the lowest rungs of the ladder. All effort must be prompted by Compassion and the determination that one's own achievements will be used for the common good. The goal must be clear and one's aspirations, prayers and mind processes must transcend thought. This I have understood to be the Highest of all Paths. Nothing must be allowed to stand in the way of achievement, and just as food itself, not the name of food, is what satisfies appetite so one must experience the Truth, not merely have an academic definition of it. And neither bodily comfort nor even bodily necessities should be allowed to stand in the way; every obstacle must be surmounted and every sacrifice, even life itself, must be willingly made.

'I can never recompense you and your Lady wife nor even thank you enough for what you have done for me. You are my benefactors. The only way I can repay you is by devoting my life to meditation to realise Nirvana at last.'

84

My feelings were so strong that I burst once more into un-premeditated song, in praise for all that I had received from my Guru and for the kindness and encouragement his wife had given me in my darkest hours.

My Master was delighted by all this and said:

'I had expected a good deal from you and I have not been disappointed.'

And his wife said:

'I knew that my son had the will and the intellect to succeed.'

Then they bade me farewell again and I went back to my cave.

Shortly after this Lama Marpa was on tour and while he was performing a ceremony he had a vision; female spirits appeared to him and reminded him of certain hints Naropa had once given him. These he had not understood at the time, but now they were interpreted to him. The upshot was that he went off again to India to see his Guru.

A few days after he had returned I myself had a dream in which a Female Spirit appeared to me and told me I lacked one particular Teaching, called the *Drong-jug*, which is a yogic treatise. When I awoke I thought over the matter, as it had been a very vivid dream and I believed the Spirit was a messenger to me, so I thought it necessary to break out of my retreat and consult my Guru about it; he would surely know everything, including this Teaching.

This I did, therefore, and pulled down my mud wall and went to him. He appeared shocked at first at my coming out of retreat, saying that it was a dangerous thing to do, but when I told him of my dream and asked to be informed whether it was a revelation or a temptation he sat silent for a while and then said:

'Yes, it is a revelation from a Higher Being. Just before I

left India my Guru Naropa spoke to me about this very Drong-jug Teaching but I do not think I ever obtained it. I will look through all my Indian manuscripts and see if it is there.'

So he and I spent the rest of the day and the best part of the night ransacking his manuscript chest but could not find the one we wanted.

'This confirms the dream I had when out on tour recently; it means I must go to India again to find this Teaching,' he said, and no amount of protests or warnings about his age and the difficult journey would deter him. Off he went, his disciples contributing freely towards the expenses.

At this time Naropa was known to have disappeared but nothing prevented my Master from following every clue in seeking him, and he would have died rather than return home with his errand unaccomplished. Eventually he ran him to earth in the jungle and they went together to a monastery where he questioned him about the Drong-jug Teaching.

'Did you recollect this yourself or did you have a revelation?' Naropa asked him.

'Neither, Sir,' Marpa replied. 'I have a disciple, one Thöpaga, to whom the revelation was granted and it was because of him that I came.'

'Excellent!' said Naropa. 'In that benighted land of Tibet there are some shining lights still to illuminate the mountain peaks!' and then he made a little chant apparently in my honour.

Naropa then gave Marpa the Oral Teaching he required and interpreted certain omens with regard to the future, deducing, for example, from the manner of Marpa's obeisance to him that his own line would die out but that he himself would be perpetuated through me. And indeed, shortly after he had returned home Marpa's only son died.

It was on the anniversary of this event after a commemoration ceremony that all the disciples begged Marpa to remember his own great age and to give them instructions as regards their respective requirements in Doctrine and Practices by means of his insight into their innate capacities, seeing he would have no successor now his son was dead.

Marpa thereupon replied: 'You know I rely upon spiritual direction obtained from omens and dreams. Go, then, my chelas, and wait upon your dreams and then come and tell me what you have seen.'

So off we all went and concentrated our minds before going to sleep, but no one else seemed to have a revelation concerning the Hierarchy. My own dream that I reported to my Guru was as follows:

'Last night I dreamed that I stood on a mountain peak in the North. The peak touched the sky and round it the sun and moon moved and illuminated with their rays all that was. The base of the mountain covered the whole earth and from its sides flowed four rivers from which all beings could drink and be satisfied. These rivers ran down into a great ocean and on its shore flowers bloomed. East of the mountain on a high pillar was a lion rampant with massive mane; its claws dug into the hillside, its head turned heavenwards; and then it left the pillar and roamed the mountainside. To the south on another pillar stood a tigress, beautifully striped, her claws sunk deep in jungle and also gazing upwards. Then she, too, roamed at will. On the west side an eagle perched upon a pillar, its wings outspread and looking up into the heavens, then took off and flew straight up into the sky. Northwards on another pillar stood a vulture, wings outspread, and on a rock was its nest with fledgling in. Upward it gazed and then high into the upper atmosphere soared the vulture. This, my Master, was my dream, I beg that you will tell us the meaning of it.'

Lama Marpa seemed highly delighted and told his wife to make a special feast, and when we were all seated he spoke:

'The Northern world is Tibet where the Buddhist Faith flourishes strongly. The mountain represents the Sect which I, Marpa the Translator, founded and to which you belong. Its peak touching the sky signifies our Goal, the sun and moon revolving are Enlightenment and Love, their illuminating rays are Grace shining upon Ignorance. The base that covers the earth shows how our deeds will fill the world; the four rivers are symbols of the Rites of Initiation and the Truths from which, all drinking, all will be eventually saved. The Ocean is the Blending of Esoteric and Fundamental Truth, the Inner and Outer Light; the flowers on the shores are Truths realised. It is a good-omened dream, my chelas.

'The eastern pillar with lion rampant is Tsurton-Wangay of Dol, a man of lion nature with a mane of Mystic Truth, his claws the claws of determination, looking up as he has renounced this life and roaming for he has gained Emancipation. The southern pillar is Ngogdun-Chudor, tigress-like, with stripes of Mystic Truths, his claws dug into the Four great duties of a Bodhisattva, looking upwards and away from the world of illusion and also roaming free, emancipated. The western pillar with soaring eagle is Meton-Tsonpo, his outspread wings the wings of Mystic Truths, having passed the pitfalls of meditation, bidden farewell to the false things of this world and soaring free. The pillar to the north with vulture perched is Thöpaga, to be known in time as Milarepa of Gungthang, with Mystic Truths imbued, his life to be as enduring as the rock on which its nest was made, the fledgling showing a peerless son; he, too, has bade farewell to normal life and has attained the great Emancipation. Chelas: this was a most excellent dream. On you falls my mantle and the Sect will prosper.'

## The Guru's Teaching

We were all overjoyed at hearing this, and then our Guru opened up all his treasured books to us and by day he instructed each individually and by night assisted us with our meditations and so our spiritual progress went on apace.

One day during a certain Initiation Rite, it occurred to Marpa to find out clairvoyantly what particular line of study was best suited to each of his four disciples who had been the pillars in my dream and so he sat down in concentration and by daybreak was able to perceive each of us in turn engaged in the correct practice, myself being observed meditating on Tum-mo or the science of generating vital heat, from which I was later to receive the name by which you know me best, Milarepa, since all those who achieve this practice earn the title of Repa, or Cottonclad ones.

Having discovered, therefore, by means of his occult powers the innate ability of each of us he then presented us with his last gift, the texts specific for our practice and his own explanation of them, and he commanded myself to go and meditate in the solitude of mountain caves far from the haunts of men.

Then before all the assembled disciples he said to us four:

'I have given each of you the texts and directions most suited to each one of you as I foretell that they will also be for your respective followers. I no longer have a son so I entrust to you all my sacred manuscripts and treasures. May you be devoted guardians of the Faith that it may prosper and spread.'

Each of the other three went to their own countries after this but my Master told me to stay with him for a few years longer yet, as he had still further Teachings to give me as well as more Initiations so that my understanding would develop the better for my remaining in his presence. At his command, I sealed myself up in a cave and the Lama and his wife sent me my share of all the food they ever had and a share from every religious ceremony. So I spent the next few years close to my Guru, in peaceful meditation, until the seeds of the Spiritual Wisdom he had planted began to shoot up in my heart.

VII

# Homesickness

We could hardly wait to hear what happened next so I asked
our Guru: 'Master, what led to your leaving Marpa and how
long did you stay in your hermitage?'

       ★       ★       ★

I did not stay very many years and it was a great wave of
nostalgia following upon a dream I had that led me to seek
permission to go home. It happened thus:

I rarely slept while meditating but one morning I had fallen
into a long and profound sleep and dreamed that I saw my
house, Four and Eight, as you will remember it was called,
broken down and dilapidated; my library was damaged by
rain leaking in through the rotten roof, and the field which
was named Worma Triangle was all overgrown with weeds.
Moreover I knew that my mother was dead and that my
sister was roving, a friendless beggar. In my sleep I burst into
tears, that my mother should have died without our having
met once again and for the unhappy lot of my sister. When
I awoke my pillow was wet. As I thought about it the longing
to see my mother grew and grew and even when awake I
wept anew. It was then I decided I must visit my family
again.

At daybreak, therefore, I pulled down the mud wall that
immured me and went to ask my Guru's permission. He was

still in bed and fast asleep when I found him and so I sat down at the head of his bed and humbly made my appeal, telling him that I could bear the separation from my loved ones no longer; would he please let me go to visit them and then I would return again quickly. Just as I finished this Lama Marpa woke. The first rays of the rising sun seeped through a chink in the shutters above his pillow making a halo round his head. At the same moment Mrs Marpa brought in his breakfast. These three events at one and the same time appeared to be an auspicious omen.

My Guru started up with an exclamation at the sight of me: 'How dare you come out of retreat suddenly like this, my son?' he demanded. 'Surely you know what risk you run? Back to your cave this moment!'

But my dream had given me courage so I told him how I had seen my house in ruins, the land overgrown and desolate, my dead mother and my sister a wandering beggarmaid. And I added that there were other people I had known I greatly desired to see yet once more, the family pastor for one and even the aunt who had treated us all so badly. Then I pleaded with him to let me go home.

My Master replied: 'My son, when you first came to me you said you had no desire for relatives or friends; now you seem to want not only these but a lot of other things as well. Even if you went home you wouldn't be likely to find your mother alive, and the others—who knows of them? You have been away a long time both here and elsewhere. But if you want to go I will give my permission.' He then proceeded to predict from omens as usual. 'If you intend to return here, the fact that you found me asleep means that we shall not meet again in this life. The sun shining on this house is a sign that you will be a shining light in the Buddhist world. The rays around my head mean that my sect shall prosper and

spread. Damema bringing in my breakfast just then means
that you will be sustained by spiritual food. Now I will let
you go. Damema,' he added to his wife, 'put offerings on the
altar.'

When all was ready he gave me the last and highest of all
Initiations and the Oral Instruction which is handed down by
word of mouth alone from Guru to chela and he warned me
to pay great attention and to hand them on only to such of
my own disciples as I should know by occult means were
ready for them.

'They must never be revealed either for gain, vanity or
from fear and coercion,' he said, 'but any chela who shows an
innate aptitude for them, him nourish and cherish and on him
bestow them. The methods of disciplining I used on you, and
Tilopa used on his chela Naropa, will not be suitable for the
degenerate beings of future generations, who will be narrow
of vision and incapable of assimilating divine Truths. Hence
beware of using them. In India there are nine texts like these.
Four of them I have given you, the other five are still somewhere in India and one of my disciples will go and try to get
them from Naropa's disciples. You, too, should do your best
to get hold of them. And in case you think I am holding
anything back because you have no offering of your own to
make, forget it; for this no longer holds between us. I am
well satisfied with your devotion and energy. To you alone
of all my disciples have I passed on the Mystic Truth whis-
pered into my ear by my Master Naropa. I repeat, to no one
else have I ever given this.' And then Marpa sang a hymn
which he made up as he went along, contrasting knowledge
and Knowledge, wealth and true spiritual Wealth, and
enjoining the renunciation of the things of this world for the
sake of Reality.

Finally my Guru laid his hand on my head lovingly and said:

'It breaks my heart that you should leave, but then all things corporeal must come to an end, so it can't be helped. Stay a few days more and study the texts and if you have anything you want explaining I can do it for you before you go.'

So I stayed for a few days and we worked through the texts.

On my last day with my beloved spiritual parents a great ceremony and feast was prepared, during which our Guru manifested himself in various divine forms with the appropriate symbols for each, and then explained that these were psycho-spiritual powers that must never be demonstrated for the mere sake of showing off or of proving one's ability. He had shown them, he said, for my benefit, as a parting gift to me. I realised then that the purpose was to point out the illusoriness of all things and I knew, too, with still greater assurance that my Guru was himself a Buddha and I made up my mind to strive to emulate him and obtain similar powers myself.

'Son,' he asked, 'have you seen and do you believe?'

'Lord and Guru,' I replied, 'it is impossible not to believe. I will do my best to become like you and obtain these powers.'

'Good!' he said in return, 'now you are well fitted to go for you know the illusoriness of the world. Go into retreat among the mountains and in caves and in places of pilgrimage; devote your whole life to meditation. Renounce all ambitions for this life and be content with the wilderness, then will you well repay your parents' love and kindness and will also serve the cause of Universal Good. But should your devotion fail then will you heap up an evil karma for yourself. So give up all worldly ambitions and don't waste time talking to the masses who are interested only in material progress, but confine yourself wholly to meditation.'

My Guru was by this time crying quite openly as he went on: 'We shall not meet again in this life, my son, but I will have your memory engraved upon my heart and mine shall be on yours, and we shall meet on higher planes when this life is finished for us both. Now I can foresee that there will come a time in your meditational career when you will be in great physical danger, so when that time comes open this scroll I am giving you and get help from it, but don't open it before then.' And he handed me a sealed scroll. I felt as if every word he had uttered was branded forever on my memory.

'Damema,' said Marpa to his wife, 'Milarepa is leaving us to-morrow so make all preparations necessary. I shall go with him a little way at the start of his journey to see him off, though I am afraid it will upset me very much.' Then he said to me: 'Sleep beside me tonight, as father with son; I want to talk.' And so I lay down beside his bed that night, although little talk was accomplished; we were both much too distressed at the thought of parting. Marpa rebuked his wife for weeping openly as she joined us, telling her that there was no cause for tears. Their son, now in possession of the Precious Truths, was off to meditate in solitude and she would do better to weep for all those benighted ones who had not the Truth and were still suffering in their ignorance. Mrs Marpa pointed out that although his reasoning was correct it didn't affect her emotions. She had lost one son and now was about to be separated from another. Wasn't that enough to make any mother weep? He and I did not do much better ourselves the short night through!

It was scarcely a merry party that set out next morning, thirteen of us all told, for those of the household accompanied me for the first four or five miles. At last, when we had reached a hill-top from which the countryside all around could be seen, we stopped and had a last meal together. When it was over my Guru took my hand and said:

'My son, I could wish that you had some companions as a guard against robbers and bandits, but it was not to be. Still, I will pray for your safety. Go carefully and be on your guard. Visit Lama Ngogdun first and with him compare notes on your texts; after that you may go on to your home. But don't stay there more than just one week and then be off into the wilds for your life of meditation, for only by this means will you benefit yourself and the rest of the world.'

In reply I extemporised a song and sang it to my Master, to assure him that, safe in the Truth, and armed with Knowledge, I should need no human comrades; the Powers above would guard and guide me. And finally I asked for his blessing. In his turn he too broke into verse beginning by assuring me of his blessing and his hopes for my spiritual future and then rendering a series of prophetic couplets foretelling what I should find at home and the nature of my life in the wilderness and ending with the blessings of all the Higher Beings and guardian deities.

Mrs Marpa, next, gave me some useful gifts suited to my material needs, such as boots, clothes and food, and then she, too, gave herself to an extemporised hymn exhorting me never to forget my spiritual parents and to continue studying and to drink deeply of all Wisdom and Knowledge; to keep always in mind the purpose of my life to help all sentient beings towards the Goal. But tears choked her before she had finished and she broke down and wept freely as I made my obeisance for the last time to the two of them. Rising, I walked away backwards that my face should be towards them as long as possible. Once out of sight I continued in the ordinary manner until reaching the top of a knoll I could look back and see the forlorn little group. I was hard put to it not to retrace my steps and stay with them forever.

But I had obtained the Teaching I had come for and had

all the Truths, and I now resolved to commit no more evil deeds. I could always meditate clearly on my Guru and he had promised we would meet again on Higher Planes. Besides, I was only going away for a short-time to see my mother and then I could come hurrying back again. Thus I tried to convince myself our parting would not be forever.

I was still consoling myself when I reached Ngogdun's house and there I stayed while we compared notes. I found he had surpassed me in one direction of study but that I was not far behind him in actual practice and, indeed, I had the last and Highest Teaching which was for Oral Transmission only, and he had not had that. So I made my obeisance to him and left for the home I had not seen for so long. The journey which normally would have taken some weeks I accomplished in three days through the practice of breath control, and I was pleased to feel my development had gone so far.

So now you know how at last I obtained the Truths and what made me leave my Master and return again to my old home.

# VIII

# Disillusionment and Renunciation

'Venerable Sir,' I now asked, 'when you reached home did you find it as you saw it in your dream and was your mother alive or not?'

'The dream was all too true,' Milarepa replied. 'I was not fated to see my mother alive again.'

'Tell us, then, Sir, of your home-coming and whom you met and how the villagers received you after so long a time had elapsed.'

★      ★      ★

Coming over the last pass I could see my house from a good distance away and on meeting with some shepherds I pretended I was a stranger. I stopped and asked them the names of different places round about and who lived in them; finally I pointed casually to Four and Eight, my own home, and inquired about it.

'Only ghosts live there now,' said one with a sad smile.

'How so?' I asked; 'what has happened to the original owners?'

'There was once a wealthy family who owned it,' I was told, 'but the father died while his only son was still a young child, and there being a flaw in the will, his father's brother and his wife did the boy and his mother out of their inheritance. When the boy grew up he demanded his rights but was

98

merely laughed at for his pains and so entered into league with the devil to get back what was rightfully his anyway. He cursed the place and launched a tremendous hail-shower and did much damage to all around. Now we are so afraid of his Powers that we scarcely dare even look at the house, much less ever go near it. His mother's body must still be inside for she died there and his sister has gone off begging after that and not been seen since. The son himself is probably dead by now; no one has heard anything of him for a very long time. If you have the courage to go there you may find books in the house.'

'How long ago did all this happen?' I asked my informant, who imagined I was a pilgrim.

'The mother died about eight years ago,' he replied, 'the hailstorm I vaguely remember when I was a child but the rest of the story is only what I have been told.'

At least I was assured that the villagers still held my memory in sufficient respect that they would not dare to harm me if they found out who I was, but I was deeply grieved at the news of my mother's death and Peta's disappearance. I hid in a dell until sunset and mourned them. When it was becoming dark I walked down into the village and there was my house—exactly as I had seen it in my dream! What had once been a magnificent country house was now a dilapidated ruin. There were my books, green with mould and soaking wet, the rain dripping down from the ceiling. Birds and mice had made their nest on the shelves and everywhere was desolation and ruin. I groped my way in the moonlight into what had been the big living-room and there saw a heap of earth and rags on the ground—for floor there was none—and grass had begun to sprout on the little hillock. Wondering what it was I felt the earth and my hand met bones. At once I knew that here was all that was left of my mother. Suddenly my

The Life of Milarepa

longing for her became intense, and I nearly fainted, but remembered in time my Guru's teachings, and instead I lay down beside the heap of bones, my head pillowed on them and went into a trance. During this trance I was able to commune with my mother's spirit and those of my guardian deities, and I realised that both my mother and my father could be assisted by me to win free from the ceaseless round of births and deaths. And one whole week I passed in this trance.

When I came out of it I had reached a sure conviction of the utter impermanence and uselessness of worldly existence so that I had not the slightest desire to follow a normal career any more. So, having decided to entrust my mother's bones to the undertaker and to give him what was left of my books in payment, I made up my mind to seek one of the caves my Master had told me of, and to sit there in solitude meditating. And should any temptation seek to lure me back to normal life I would commit suicide rather than yield to it.

This, then, was my firm resolve.

Examining my books, therefore, I found that though the bindings were ruined the letters were still clear and readable, so making a bundle of them I slung it on my back and carrying my mother's bones in my arms I went to look for our old family pastor, making up a poem on the way, reiterating my firm conviction in the transience and illusoriness of life and worthlessness of its so-called pleasures. And I renewed my resolve to seek the Truth in meditation far from the haunts of human beings.

When I came to our pastor's house I found that he was dead; but his son was there, who said he would see to the matter of my mother's bones for me. He was at first afraid to take the books lest my old curse should go with them. When I assured him on this point he accepted them and together we performed the necessary ceremony for my mother's funeral. When we were finished the young man wanted me to stay so that we could talk over old times together, but I told him I had to go off at once and had no time for talking. However, he insisted that I stayed the night so that he could collect together some provision for me and to this I consented.

He was greatly struck at my switch over from the Black Arts to being a religious devotee and asked what Guru I had found and what I had learned. I recounted some of my experiences with Marpa and how, in the end, I had received the Initiation of the Great Perfection. He congratulated me and suggested I should repair my house and marry Zesay, to whom I was still betrothed, and settle down as a Lama. I explained that Marpa had married so as best to be able to serve others but that if I tried to imitate him without having reached his state of spiritual evolution it would be like a hare trying to imitate a lion's leap. All I wanted, I said, was a life of meditation in solitude, caring no longer for the things of this world, and this had been my Master's command so this was what I must do. By this means, I explained, I could save not only my father and mother but many other beings as well and benefit myself into the bargain. The sight of the desolation and ruin of my old home had brought home to me as nothing else could have the utter worthlessness of possessions and nothing, not even slow starvation, would make me alter my decision now.

And then once again, as always when I was deeply moved in spirit, I burst into song, opening with salutation to my Master and calling upon him to further me in my determination to avoid attachment to the things of the world. All was illusory, henceforth I would seek the contemplative life.

My host and his wife were much moved by my song and over and over again I repeated to myself my resolve to devote my life to meditation and to think nothing of the pleasures of the world. And I assure you, Rechung and the rest of my disciples, I have never regretted it nor wished that instead I had wasted my time in worldly pursuits and ambitions.

## IX

# The Wilderness

I begged our Master that he tell us now of the places he visited and stayed in and what he meditated on and how he practised.

*      *      *

Next morning our old pastor's son gave me some food including a sack of flour, some cheese and butter, and offered them with the request that I should remember him and his wife during my meditations; so I departed and the first cave I sought was one in the hillside quite close behind my own house. Deep in my devotions I ate sparingly and the food lasted me for some months, but I became quite weak. When there was nothing left I decided I should have to go out and beg or I would not be able to continue. So I set out with my begging bowl towards the cottages and shacks of herdsmen who lived in the hills.

The first dwelling I came to was a yak-skin tent and putting my head in saw that, as luck would have it, I had hit upon—of all people's—my aunt's tent! Of course she recognised me immediately and promptly let loose the dogs on me, which I had to keep off with my staff and by throwing stones at them. Thereupon out she came herself, armed with a tent-pole, and proceeded to beat me unmercifully, the while hurling abuse and raillery at me:

'You disgrace to your noble father! You murderer of your

own kinsmen! You ruination of the countryside! What have you come here for? To think that your father could have begotten a son like you!'

And she struck me again and again so that I turned to run away, but being weak for lack of food I stumbled against a stone and fell into a pool of water and nearly drowned. Struggling out of it somehow while my aunt still hurled abuse at me, I managed to prop my weakened body up on my staff. Then, in deep grief, I sang a song to my aunt, who actually stopped her reviling to listen. In it I related how she and my uncle were the cause of much suffering to two orphan children and their widowed mother. While the one child had gone off as a mendicant, the mother had died in poverty, the sister had strayed away no one knew whither. The family thus broken up and lost to each other, I had taken up a life of solitude to meditate upon the teachings of my Guru but my supply of food being exhausted I had emerged from my retreat merely to restock in order to keep alive. I had somehow been lured to my aunt's door and she had set the dogs on me and flogged my already emaciated frame with a tent-pole. However, although I had cause for anger against her, yet, mindful of my Master's Teachings I would allow no such feelings to enter my mind nor plan any vengeance; let Marpa himself help me to keep down my wrath!

This song caused a servant girl who was standing behind my aunt to burst into tears, and even my aunt herself was somewhat conscience-stricken and ashamed of herself. So she went into her tent again and sent me out a roll of butter and some cheese-flour by the girl. Continuing my interrupted round of other tents and shacks I could not recognise anybody, but they all seemed to know me at once; although they stared hard they were generous in their donations of food, and I was able to return to my cave well provisioned.

# The Wilderness

Having experienced my aunt's reactions I could imagine what my uncle's would be and intended to avoid his dwelling, but he had built himself a new house. This, of course, I did not know, so I had gone right up to the door before a stone well aimed made me realise my mistake. 'I've been waiting a long time to meet you,' he cried, as he rushed out pelting me with more stones. I turned and ran hard, but he then seized his bow and arrows and began shooting at me wildly crying out to the neighbours that at last they had the destroyer of their countryside in their grasp; they had but to catch him.

It seemed I would be lynched then and there. In desperation I cried out to my Guru, calling upon him by name, and on my guardian deities to save me from my enemies. This had the effect of stopping my pursuers who were still, apparently, in mortal fear of my magic powers; they laid hold of my uncle and prevented him from harming me any more, and in their panic they even gave me alms. Not so my uncle, who remained staunchly aggressive although rendered impotent by the young men who held him back.

On returning to my cave I decided it would be best to leave the district next day as there was still so much hostility to me, but that night I had a dream which made me stay a few days longer.

It happened then that Zesay, the girl to whom I had been betrothed as a child, came to hear of my arrival and visited my cave with delicacies of food and drink. She embraced me tearfully and told me details of my mother's death and my sister's straying which filled me with grief.

'You have remained very faithful, being still unmarried,' I remarked.

'People were so afraid of your Powers that no one dared to ask for my hand,' she said with a faint smile, 'but anyway, I wouldn't have married if anyone had proposed. It is a very good thing that you have taken to the religious life, but what are you going to do about your house and lands?'

I knew what she was after and as I had given up all claim to worldly possessions I said:

'If you see my sister Peta, tell her I give them to her. Until she turns up again you can have the use of them. And if Peta has died then they are for you altogether.'

'Don't you want them yourself?' she asked wonderingly.

'I find my food wherever it may be or else starve, so what use is a field to me. I dwell only in caves and mountain retreats so what would I do with a house? I have learned that even if I owned the whole world, I could not take it with me when I died, so I shall be much happier both here and here-after if I give everything up now. It is certainly the opposite way round from the way most people think and act, but still, just forget that I am alive.'

'Is your practice different from that of all other religious persons, too?' she asked.

'Naturally I am opposed to those hypocrites who become monks for the respect and honour they get from their monkish garb,' I replied, 'while still trying to amass wealth and fame, for thus they are trying to have the best of both worlds. They learn a book or two of the Scriptures by heart and then dis-solve into unseemly religious party strife. But the really sincere seekers after Truth and Religion, whatever their party or creed, if they do not do like these others, then they must be men after my own heart and there can really be little difference between us. In short, what I feel is, any who are not sincere are of a different creed from me and any who are, whatever religious label they may wear, are of the same faith.'

'How is it, then, that your own form of practice makes you appear even inferior to a common beggar. I have never seen

anyone looking as you do before. To what sect or creed do
you belong?'

I told her that it was to the Path of Total Self-Abnegation
by which one can attain to Buddhahood in a single lifetime,
but for this all worldly aims and ambitions must be scattered
to the four winds.

'H'm,' she said doubtfully, 'your ideas and theirs seem very
different and the Path that you have taken very difficult.'

'Theirs is easier to tread, certainly,' I said, 'but a yogi who
still clings to his attachments is not my idea of a true devotee.
Even sincere seekers who cannot part with their yellow robes
retain a little love for the things of this world, especially of
fame and honour, and even if they have given them up there
is still a vast difference between the saffron-robed monk and
myself in the speed and efficacy of the attainment of Buddhahood. But you won't understand that just yet. So, if you can,
devote yourself to a religious life, if not go home and enjoy
my one-time property.'

'I cannot accept the house and grounds that rightfully belong to your sister. I should like to be a devotee—but not a
devotee like you!' And with that she left me.

Of course it came to my aunt's ears that I had ceased to have
any interest in my property and thinking that, since I had
avowedly followed the commands of my Guru, she might be
able to have them legally now, she came to see me and brought
a quantity of food and drink with her as an offering. Approaching in humble fashion entirely unlike her usual self, she said:

'I treated you very roughly last time we met, nephew;
please put it down to my ignorance and forgive me as befits
a religious person like yourself. Suppose now I cultivate your
field for you and keep you supplied with food?'

'All right,' I answered, 'bring me twenty measures of
barley a month and you can have all the rest.'

So off she went well pleased with her day's work. For two months the barley arrived and then one day she herself turned up at the mouth of my cave again and said:

'People are saying that if I cultivate your field your Tutelary Deities will be offended and harm us again.'

'Why should I practise Black Magic any more?' I asked. 'You will be making up a little for all your wickedness if you cultivate my field for me and keep me supplied.'

She at once said:

'Please, then, will you take an oath that you won't practise your spells any more?'

An innocent in the ways of the world, I took the oath she required and she went away again even more delighted than before.

Now all this time I had been persevering in meditation, but was unable to obtain signs of any improvement or growth in my knowledge or experience of the Yoga of Body Heat. This naturally depressed me and made me worry about what I should do next. It was then, one night, that I had a dream. I was ploughing a field but the soil was so hard that I could make no impression on it; I was in despair when my Guru Marpa, himself, appeared and urged me to persevere. He himself guided the oxen so that the earth turned up easily and a rich harvest followed. This gave me great pleasure.

At first the thought arose that dreams were only one's own illusory thoughts after all and that even fools would not allow them to have any effect, but then it seemed to me to be giving me a definite message from my Master. The better to impress it on my memory, I made my dream into a poem. I likened the hard soil to my mind on which faith shed water and manure to nourish it and Grace fell as a shower of rain. The oxen and plough were Concentration, the share was the Right Method and Reason; the guiding hand was Purpose

and the whip was zeal and perseverance. Thus would the
hardened soil of Ignorance be broken and the stones of sin
and weeds of hypocrisy be rooted out. The harvest, of course,
was the Good Life achieved with the Fruits of Truth to be
picked.

I decided to go and find another of the caves that Marpa
had told me I should occupy some time and I was about to
start out when I saw my aunt climbing up the hill complete
with sixty measures of barley, a ragged coat of skins, a roll of
good cloth and some butter in a ball. These she threw down at
my feet and said:

'Here you are, nephew, these are in payment for your
field. Now get out of my sight and as far away from here as
you can. The neighbours are all saying that that Thöpaga will
do us mischief again if I have any truck with him. And they
are ready to kill us both. So it is safer for you to make your
escape while the going's good. I don't see why they should
kill me but they certainly will kill you if you stay.'

I knew well enough that people were not saying anything
of the sort, for it was not the sort of thing they would say, and
I realised now how I had been had by the taking of the oath.
However I replied:

'Aunt, if I were not faithful to my vows I would pulverise
you into a corpse this moment, for these circumstances alter
the taking of my oath. But if I do not practise patience upon
people like you who insist upon harming me, on whom else
shall I practise it? Yet what use is the field to me? If I should
die tonight I could not enjoy it any more. But Patience is a
sure Path to Buddhahood and therefore of much more value
than that field. Also, you and Uncle have been the cause of
my taking up a religious life so for this I am grateful to you
and will pray for you that even you, too, may reach Buddhahood in your next lives. You have taken the field; I give you

the house also.' And then I expounded the Doctrine to her and ended with a song illustrating the contrast between the worldly life of wealth, pleasure, food and drink—particularly the latter which inhibits all Spiritual Growth—and that of the ascetic, who is free of the fetters that have bound him to the world.

'A truly religious person should be like you, nephew,' said my aunt, as she walked away well satisfied.

I was very much upset that she could have behaved thus but at the same time I was glad to be rid of the responsibility of ownership. I determined to carry out my plan and to find the other cave I had in mind. So next morning with my aunt's so-called payment and what little was left of my own provisions I set out and in due course found the place and made myself comfortable; putting my bedding on a hard mattress on the ground. I took a vow then and there not to descend into human habitations again until I had attained the Power that I was seeking, the super-normal Knowledge that is the prelude to Enlightenment, and I prayed to my deities to assist me in keeping this vow. Should I break them, I prayed that I might die immediately.

And so I continued for a long time living on a little of the flour with whatever other food there happened to be and I grasped the knowledge of the Highest Initiation I had been given. But my body had become by then too weak to control the Psycho-Physical Fluid or Power so that I could still not acquire the Inner Heat and remained very sensitive to the cold.

Then I prayed with great earnestness to my Guru and as the result there came to me a vision of a number of female spirits who said they had been sent by Lama Marpa. They performed a religious ceremony and afterwards gave me instructions in certain exercises. As I practised these later I began to feel generating in myself the Psychic Heat, and I continued hard at work on this for another year.

Quite suddenly there came over me a desire to go out and find some form of recreation. I was actually on the point of setting out when I remembered my vows and stopped in time, rebuking myself soundly for even having had such a thought, much less having all but yielded to it. Then I sang myself a song of self-reproof reminding that unworthy mortal, Milarepa, that he was fortunate in being alone and undisturbed by the cares of the world, and what business had he to feel lonely all of a sudden. If he did but let his mind rest in peace, tempting thoughts would not enter it. Great were the dangers to be met with by a devotee who returned to the world, and all for what?

And so for yet another three years I continued my meditation and developed in spiritual knowledge not a little in that time. But my stock of barley flour was by now exhausted despite my stringent ration of only twenty measures of flour per year, and it began to look as if I would die of starvation without having obtained Buddhahood. It occurred to me how people in the world become so happy in a moment when they find a shilling and are so unhappy if they lose one. Compared with that form of transient happiness my life was ideal and Buddhahood more valuable than a million shillings. Indeed, it would be better to die in the process of keeping my vows than to break them. What was I to do? Then I thought it would not be breaking vows to seek food if I did not go to human habitation; it was that that I had foresworn.

One morning, therefore, I strolled out beyond the mouth of my cave and came upon a sunny spot where there was a spring and plenty of nettles growing around, as picturesque a place as one could wish and commanding a wide view over the countryside. So delighted was I with this that I moved

my few possessions out of the cave and down to the spring
and there continued my meditation, living on soup made from
nettles and nothing else.

My body had shrunk to no more than its skeleton, greenish
in colour the parchment skin and even the hair turned green.
No clothes had I by then to cover the outside nor any proper
food within. The scroll which my Guru had given me to
consult in an emergency, I used to take down and look at
lovingly and place it on my head as a sign of my respect for
what was written therein, as is the custom with us Tibetans;
and this seemed to ease the pangs of hunger even though I had
nothing to eat. Sometimes, even, I would belch afterwards
as if I had just finished a good meal. Once or twice I very
nearly opened it, but something prevented me for I knew it
was not the time for so doing. My danger must be greater
still. But ever it lay beside me.

Another year passed and some hunters came wandering by,
having failed to find any game. At first sight of me they fled, for
they thought I must be an evil spirit. I assured them, however, I was a human being like themselves and a religious
devotee.

'You don't look like one!' was their comment, but they
were sufficiently reassured to come and take a closer look at
the weird object. Then they went into my cave and pried
into every nook and cranny of it. Finding nothing they came
out again and down to my spring and asked:

'Where is your food store? Let us have some and we will
pay you back all right. But if you won't give us anything we
will kill you.'

'I have nothing but nettles,' I replied. 'And even had I anything else I would not give it to anyone so rude as yourselves,
who demand things by force.'—They had particularly in-
sulted me by lifting me up.

'We're not trying to rob you,' they protested, 'and what do we gain by insulting you?'

'You might possibly gain some merit,' I remarked.

They were quick to reply: 'All right, we'll insult you over and over again,' and they suited the action to the words and picked me up and dropped me several times, so that my unprotected bones were badly bruised and I felt much pain.

One of them, however, who had refused to take part in this baiting of me, said: 'Look here, you fellows, this chap seems to be a real Saint, and even if he isn't you aren't doing yourselves any good by bullying a weak person who can't protect himself. It's not his fault that we're hungry, so stop it now!' Then he said to me: 'Hermit, you are a very good man to tolerate such treatment. As I have not done anything to you myself, please remember me in your prayers.'

The others took this as a joke and said: 'Yes, remember us too for having lifted you up and down.'

'Aye, that he will, you may be quite sure,' the first one added, 'but it will be in a different way!' Roaring with laughter they went off.

I certainly did not curse them, but apparently retribution overtook them. I heard long afterwards that they had been arrested by the Governor of the Province, the leader was killed and the rest had their eyes put out as punishment, all except the one who had spoken kindly on my behalf.

Another year passed and all the dress I had consisted of some rags of the cloth which my aunt had given me and the sack the flour had been in. The tattered skin served as a bedspread and folded over the lower part of my body, the sack I laid over my chest and with what was left of the rags I covered the essential parts of me. Then this seemed to be going beyond the bounds of self-abnegation and I knotted the rags together to form three pieces tied together with a bit of rope I found;

and this was my daytime dress while at night there was the
skin and sack. But I still felt the cold.

Still another year went by when one day I heard the sound
of voices and peeping out of my cave I saw quite a crowd of
people carrying game which they had shot. When the foremost of the party saw me they dropped the baggage with a
cry of: 'Look out! There's a Spirit!' and fled. But those
behind who could not see laughed at them and said that one
did not find Spirits in broad daylight. 'Take another look!'
they added, being themselves at a safe distance. 'It's there
still!' was the confirmation made in frightened tones and then
even those furthest in the rear began to be afraid. So out I went
and told them I was no Spirit, only a hermit who was reduced
to this condition from lack of food. Not satisfied they ransacked the cave but finding only nettles they were filled with
awe and reverence. They left me a large store of their meat
and said in most respectful voices: 'You are indeed a good man
to practise asceticism like this. Please pray for the animals we
have killed and for our own sin in having killed them.'

The thought of having some ordinary food as one normally
eats, once again, was truly wonderful and as I ate of it a feeling
of well-being and comfort spread over me so that I was able
to apply my mind all the more to my exercises and I reached
a state of bliss such as I had not before known. Great must
have been the merit those good people had acquired by giving
food to a strange old hermit on a hillside, more than if they
had given the richest gifts to the well-to-do who lived in
towns. I rationed myself with the meat until at last, before it
was finished it became maggoty. I debated whether to clear
the maggots off but felt that that would be tantamount to
committing a robbery, depriving the maggots of their food, so
I left the remainder to them and returned to my nettle soup.

One night someone who thought I had hidden wealth came

and stealthily ransacked my cave, going into every corner, searching. At this I laughed outright and remarked: 'If you can find anything at night which I haven't managed to find in the daylight, you deserve to keep it.' At which he laughed too and left.

After about a year another party of hunters came strolling past the cave. I was sitting in a trance attired in my three rags and the bit of rope so they prodded me with the ends of their bows to see if I was a human being or not. From the state of my body and my 'clothes' they had provisionally decided against it.

While they were discussing my possible nature I opened my mouth and said: 'Of course I'm a man.'

Then one asked: 'Are you Thöpaga?'

When I admitted it they asked me for the loan of some food, assuring me they would repay it handsomely. 'We heard that you had come home some years ago,' they said. 'Have you been here all this time?'

'I have,' I replied, 'but I cannot give you any food for I haven't any you could eat.'

'Ah! Whatever does for you does for us; we aren't particular,' they said.

'Make a fire, then, and gather nettles and put them into boiling water,' I said, and this they did. When the broth was boiling merrily one said:

'Let's have the meat or bones for stock, or some fat.'

'If I had that,' I replied, 'I should have quite tasty food.'

'Then give us the flour or some sort of grain for thickening,' they asked hopefully.

'If I had that I would have quite nutritional food,' I told them, 'and I haven't had any such for years. Try nettle-tips instead.'

'Well, at least give us some salt,' they asked in desperation.

I repeated my previous answers and recommended nettle-tips.

'If you live on this sort of so-called food and wear those bits of rags and rope, no wonder you look like you do. Why, you are hardly human. If you got no better job than that of a servant you would at least have some decent food to put inside you. You're the most miserable looking specimen of humanity ever and the most pitiable.'

'Now don't say that,' I protested. 'It's just the opposite. I'm far and away the most lucky for I met with Marpa the Great Translator who became my Teacher and I learned from him the Truth by which one can obtain Buddhahood in one lifetime. Hence out of the whole of humanity I am the only one with real courage and true ambition. As for you—born into a Buddhist country you have never listened even to one religious discourse in all your lives and you have set your aim at the lowest of all possible worlds and a long term therein! You are piling up a big debit account against yourselves. You have such a wrong sense of values. In contrast, I am happy in the prospect of my future Bliss and enjoy those things which are truly productive of happiness. The attainment of Buddhahood is worth far, far more than clothes or food, and my scanty possessions are enough for keeping me alive. Do as I do. But if you cannot see the error of your ways then at least spare me your pity. Evening is coming on, the sun is going down. It is time you were off to your homes, and as death overtakes each one of us I must not waste time on useless talk so I am going back to my meditation now.'

This last part I rendered, as was my usual habit, in verse. Instead of taking to heart my words they said:

'You've really got a very good voice, you know. Well, we can't rough it like you're doing so we will leave you.' And off they went.

116

However, their visit was not without its aftermath. Remembering my song and the tune, they happened to sing it at a public holiday festival at which, by chance, my sister Peta was begging. When she heard it she said: 'Gentlemen, that man you sing of must be a veritable Buddha,' at which they laughed uproariously and chaffed her for praising her own brother.

'Buddha or no,' said one, 'it's your own brother who is fading away from sheer starvation.'

'How can you gloat over my miseries like that?' she cried, 'my parents are long since dead, my brother disappeared and I am reduced to begging.' And she dissolved into passionate weeping.

Zesay came upon her just at that point and stopped to comfort her, suggesting that they might not be making fun of her and that it could be me after all. 'I also saw him some time ago. Go to the cave and see if he is still there. If so then we will both visit him.'

Now more convinced she arrived at the mouth of my cave with some light beer in one hand and a bag of flour in the other, but the first sight of me frightened her. My bony skeleton stood out a mass of ridges and points, my eyes were sunk far into their sockets, my skin was still of greenish-blue, my muscles had atrophied almost completely, the hair on my head stuck straight up, and my limbs seemed as frail as matchsticks. Naturally, therefore, I gave her a dreadful shock and she thought at first I was some sort of ghost. But then she remembered she had heard I was dying of starvation and mustered up the courage to approach and ask me: 'Are you a man or a ghost?'

'I am Mila Thöpaga,' I replied, and at the sound of my voice she flung herself at me and embraced me, calling me 'Brother!' Then she fainted away. It took me a bit of time to bring her round again but when I managed to she put her head on my knees and burst into a flood of tears.

'Our mother died, longing for a sight of you,' she sobbed. 'No one came near us and I could not bear to be alone in that big house with no means of support, and so I took to begging my way through distant country. I thought you, too, must be dead by now. But as you're alive I am very surprised to find you are not in better circumstances than these. You see how my Fate pursues me! Where is anyone more unhappy than myself?' And she gave herself over to self-pity and lamentation, calling upon our parents. I did my best to console her.

Being affected by her misery I relieved my feelings once more by singing. I began by reiterating my vow to solitude and then compared my sister's longings for material welfare with my own for Enlightenment. I was content with whatever Nature had to offer just so long as it led to my gaining Transcendent Knowledge which would mean that in my next birth I would be born into Buddhahood.

'If all this were true,' said Peta, 'it would be wonderful, but I just can't believe it. If it were, surely all devotees would practise as hard as you do, but I have never seen, in all my wanderings, anyone who is as ascetic as yourself.' She then gave me the food and drink she had brought and departed. How I enjoyed it! With much greater vigour I was able to plunge back into my meditations that night.

But the next morning my body got the better of me and I suffered a great longing to sample again the comforts of the world, so much that it was accompanied by actual physical pain. No amount of effort at concentrating was of any avail to me in this mood.

A few days later Zesay came to visit me bringing Peta with her and armed with well-cured meat, beer and butter and flour. They met me when I was on my way to the spring for water and I was by now stark naked. They were both acutely embarassed and yet were moved to tears by my poverty.

I was drinking some of the beer when Peta said:

'Brother, however I look at you you don't seem to me to be quite a normal human being. Please do take to begging and eat proper food fit for a man. I will try to get hold of a bit of cloth for you to cover yourself with meanwhile.'

And Zesay added her entreaties too: 'Yes, do take to begging for alms,' she said, 'and I also will come with a bit of cloth for you.'

'Seeing one never knows when death may overtake one,' I pointed out, 'I don't see the use of wasting valuable time on begging. Even if I were to die of cold it would be for the sake of the Truth. I could never be satisfied with the outward show of religion as practised by a merry gathering who revel freely in food and drink and wearing the most expensive and best tailored garments—all at the expense of real devotion. I need neither your cloths nor your visits. And I will pay no attention to your advice about going begging.'

Peta then asked: 'How can you ever be satisfied then? For to my mind you must ever be yearning after a condition even worse than the one you are in and be trying to devise more and more mortifications for the flesh than those you are at present indulging in? Or does even your ingenuity fail to produce any further ones?'

'There are three states of existence worse still than mine,' I replied: 'the world of animals, the world of ghosts and Hell. And most people seem to be striving their best to get themselves born into one or other of these as far as I can see. No, I'm quite satisfied with my present state of affairs.' And then I sang them the song of my contentment in my life of solitude.

'Certainly you practise what you preach,' said Zesay when they had listened to it. 'One can't help admiring you.'

'Whatever you may say, brother,' Peta objected, 'I cannot go on seeing you naked and starving. I will do my best to get that bit of cloth for you and bring it over. Your devotion would not run away for your having enough food and clothes. But if you refuse to go out begging for alms it looks as if you will get your wish and die in your solitude from cold and want. Still, if you don't go and die too soon I will bring you that cloth just as soon as I can get hold of some.' Then the pair of them left me.

Unfortunately the good food increased my physical pains and mental disturbances so much that I was unable to go on with my meditation. In this awkward dilemma I felt the moment had come for opening the scroll my Master had given me, for what greater danger is there for anyone than to have put his hand to the plough and then to start looking back?

And lo! Within that scroll was the solution to my exact problem! There was written the diagnosis of my complaint and the treatment by which the danger could not only be averted but turned to good account. Further it was written on the scroll that at this time I should take good plain food and it explained my trouble to me; that my determined and prolonged meditation had attuned my nerves to a changed mode of function but that the change had been retarded by lack of food. Peta's beer had then excited my nerves and the unaccustomed food had also affected them. Now I understood what was happening in my body as well as my mind and I entered upon the new exercises I found in the scroll with vigour, practising them hard. I began to experience a state of calmness and clarity of vision that is above the physical plane, and was like to what I had reached before, but this time it far exceeded my previous efforts in the depth and intensity of my ecstasy. Thus did a hitherto unknown and Transcendent Knowledge come into me. It was obvious to me that my tendency to evil had been turned to good in the nick of time and I began to comprehend the Oneness of the All which annihilates the subject-object relationship in terms of which we normally think all our lives. Both Nirvana and the World of Illusion I now saw were but relative and dependent states and that there was nought but Mind in which there is no distinction, no separateness. Following the idea of Mind as Universal Cause in the ordinary direction one comes to the World of Illusion that men normally perceive; in the opposite direction it leads to Nirvana, or the comprehension of such illusion and Perception without any illusory base. Both our world and Nirvana I perceived lay in the Concept of the Void (the non-existence of Space) which is Mind.

This new Knowledge I had gained was born of my previous intense efforts. All that I had needed at the crisis was nourishment and directions, and now I had both. And to this Peta and Zesay had materially contributed so my debt to them was very great indeed. I dedicated a hymn to their good act so that it would be consecrated to the Eternal Purpose.

After further intensive practice and meditation there began to develop in me certain Powers, those of transforming myself into any shape I desired and of being able to fly through the air. By day, then, I could work seeming miracles and by night I could traverse the Universe in every plane and could see all that it held. At first these Powers manifested themselves only in my dreams but as I went on eventually I found I was actually able to fly in broad daylight and go where I would to meditate, and this led to my greater progress in the Art of Developing Vital Heat, which was my main aim.

One day I was flying thus and was passing over a village where lived a distant relative of mine whose daughter-in-law had been one of the thirty-five killed at the collapse of my uncle and aunt's house. He and his son were out ploughing the field as I floated over them, the son being at the oxen's head and the father guiding the ploughshare.

The son happened to look up and saw me and cried: 'Look, there's a man flying!'

'What of it?' said the father angrily. 'Why are you standing there like one moonstruck? It's only that rogue Mila, a good-for-nothing starveling, son of a wicked woman from near here. Out of the way and don't get under his shadow and carry on with your job.' The father was dodging about at the time too trying to avoid being covered by my shadow. But his son answered him back:

'I don't mind whether a man is good for nothing or not just so long as he can fly; that's a most wonderful thing for a man to be able to do.' And he went on gazing up at me!

It now seemed as if I had really reached a stage when I might be of use in helping all sentient beings but I had had the express command from my Guru to confine myself to meditation only as being the best form of service I could give humanity and the Buddhist Faith. However, if I stayed where I was when it was known that I could fly, people would come flocking to me to see me work miracles and fame and prosperity would impede any further progress. So I decided to move to the slopes of Mount Everest where caves were numerous and off I set with my sole possession, my earthenware pot in which I cooked my nettle soup, on my back.

But I was weak and unaccustomed to walking by now so that I slipped on a stone even as I was leaving my cave, and the pot fell and broke. When it did the lining of green scum separated from it and fell apart like another pot, complete.

# The Wilderness

This stressed very much to my mind the impermanence of all material things and I took it as an omen that I was to continue my devotions. I sat down and composed a hymn to my new Guru, the Pot, which had taught me such a lesson.

I was still singing it when some hunters passed by and stopped to listen. Then one said:

'Hermit, you have a very fine singing voice. What are you doing there with a broken pot and its green scum lining? And how is it you yourself are of greenish hue too and so emaciated?'

I told them and they gazed at me wonderingly and then invited me to share a meal with them. During it one of the younger ones remarked:

'You seem to be a man of powerful physique—or were once. You would make an excellent soldier, armed and on horseback. You would become rich, too, and could rescue your relatives and be really happy. Or you might be a successful merchant and earn plenty. At the worst you could go into service and be sure of good food and clothes. Up to now this doesn't seem to have occurred to you, but start thinking about it now.'

But one of the older and wiser said: 'He seems to be a very great devotee and is not likely to listen to any material wisdom that we can offer him. Better keep quiet.' Then he said to me: 'Please sing us another song and teach us a lesson by it.'

'You all seem to think I am a miserable and unhappy specimen,' I replied, 'but actually there's no one in the world happier than myself nor anyone who has made a greater success of life than I have, but you would never be able to understand that. I will sing you a song of the things I enjoy as much as you enjoy any of your type of pleasures. Just listen to it.'

123

And with that I sang them The Yogi's Song. In effect it went thus:

'Within the Temple of my Body, within the breast where the altar is, the Horse of Mind is prancing about. What lassoo must be used to catch this Horse? To what post must it be tied? What food must be given it? What drink should it have and where must it be put for warmth? The Lassoo is Singleness of Purpose; the Post is Meditation; its Food is the Guru's Teaching; its drink is the Stream of Consciousness; and the Enclosure for it in cold weather is The Void. For Saddle use the Will; for Bridle the Intellect; its Girths are Fixedness and its Headstall and Noseband are The Vital Airs. Its Rider is Mindfulness; the Helmet that he wears is Altruism; his Coat of Mail is Learning and Contemplation. On his back is the Shield of Patience and in his hand the Spear of Aspiration. By his side hangs the Sword of Intelligence; his Arrows are the shafts of Universal Mind made straight by absence of hate and anger and barbed with the Feathers of the Four Great Virtues, tipped with the Arrowhead of Keen Understanding. The pliant Bow is Spiritual Wisdom fixed in the Aperture of Right Method and the Right Path. These Arrows drawn to the Full Extent of Humanity, when shot fall among all the nations; and they strike those who are Faithful and kill the Selfish Spirit. Thus are all Evil Passions overcome and protected is all mankind, our kindred. The Horse gallops along the broad Plain of Happiness with the state of Buddhahood as Goal. Behind it it leaves Attachments to the things of the world, ahead of it lies Deliverance. Such is the course I am tending towards Buddhahood. Now, think you this is your idea of Happiness? For worldly happiness I have no use.'

They heard me and I believe I made some impression on them as they left, having strengthened their faith. And now, quite unburdened, I continued on my journey until I reached a spot which commanded a magnificent view; here I stopped a while and lay down by the roadside to drink it in.

As I lay there a party of young girls came by and seeing me one cried out: 'Goodness, what a terrible looking specimen of a man that is! God grant I may never be born like that.' And another said: 'How dreadful. It makes me frightened to look at him.'

Thinking what poor ignorant creatures they were, I got up in pity for them and remonstrated with them thus: 'Now then, girls, don't talk like that. There's nothing for you to worry about at all for you would never be born like me if you tried for a hundred years or more. It is a good thing to feel pity, but pity and self-conceit should not be allies for that is not consistent. Now listen to this song.' I burst out once more into melody, showing how the whole world has a perverted sense of values and no one cares for any but himself. I assured them that our pity was mutual but that mine for them was based on knowledge. I also told them my name that they might know with whom they had to deal.

When it was finished the girl who had pitied me was ashamed and said to her companions: 'This is the famous Milarepa and we have spoken very foolishly in our conceit; let us now ask his pardon.' This she did, making a prostration and offering me some currency, begging me to sing again to them for their good. This I did to oblige her and continued my previous theme on different Values and how a rake is thought more of in this world than a religious devotee. In the end I pardoned them for their presumption and thanked her for her offering.

I went on until I reached a cave known locally as 'Sunny Castle' and there I spent some months progressing well with my meditational practice and being kept supplied in food and drink by the country folk round about. Although

satisfactory for a time this, I knew, could only lead to retro-
gression of my development from distraction and over-
popularity, so I thought up the list of the caves my Guru had
mentioned and set off once again, this time towards Mount
Everest.

Just before I started out Peta came, having been looking for
me with a piece of blanket cloth she had managed to appropriate. She had been to my old cave and found me gone and
on making inquiries heard at one village that a hermit who
looked like a caterpillar had passed that way. She followed
my path until she found me. On the way she had seen a
magnificent Lama, one Bari-Lotsa-wa, who occupied a raised
dais under a large umbrella, and was arrayed in silks of many
colours; he was surrounded by disciples who blew conch
shells to attract people's attention, and all around this Lama
milled men and women with offering. When she saw this
Peta had thought: 'Why can't my brother be like this? Other
people enjoy their religion, his is sheer purgatory to him as
well as being a shame to his relations. If I can meet him I will
try and persuade him to become a disciple of this Lama.'
Further inquiries of the townsfolk elicited the information that
I had been seen in the district and so she eventually arrived at
my new dwelling-place, full of good intentions and with her
piece of cloth.

'Now look here,' she started on me immediately, 'you
really can't go on living like this, naked and starving and calling it a religious life. You're not only shameless; you're
positively indecent! Make a skirt of this blanket and then go
to this Lama Bari-Lotsa-wa who is a very great Lama, quite
different from you. He sits on a throne under an umbrella,
dressed in silk robes, and he's always drinking tea or beer. He
is surrounded by disciples and lay followers and they walk in
front of him wherever he goes, blowing trumpets and shells.

Everywhere he is a crowd gathers and they bring offerings worth having. He certainly can be thought of as a great Lama. I want you to go and try to become his disciple. Even if you are the lowest of the low in his retinue, still that would be better than your present condition. We can't go on with your devotion to poverty and my habitual bad luck. We shall just die.' And her feelings overcame her and she burst into tears.

Once again I had to start explaining the perverted sense of values held by her in common with the rest of mankind, in order to try to comfort her.

'Don't talk like this, Peta,' I said: 'you are ashamed of my being naked. But I am proud of having obtained the Truth which I could not have done had I not been a man, so I can see no shame in my body. I was born like this. Let those feel ashamed who do evil deeds and break their parents' hearts, covet what has been devoted to religious usage and who are utterly unscrupulous in obtaining their selfish ends, regardless of what pain and suffering it may cause others. They alone need to feel shame. But if you feel ashamed at seeing my body with which I was born, what about your breasts, which you were not born with but only acquired later, and which are now quite prominently displayed? Also, if you think I meditate in poverty just because I am unable to get a job or earn any money, you're wrong. It is the world of illusion and its trammels that I fear to get caught up in. I feel the pain and suffering of the world as if flames were scorching my skin. I loathe the thought of worldly possessions and the craving for them that develops, even as a bilious man loathes the sight and thought of rich food. That is why I am like I am. Moreover my Guru Marpa the Translator, told me to give up all worldly concerns and possessions, to do without food, clothing or even a name; to live in solitude and to practise my devotions with energy and perseverance. Seeing that this was my Guru's command, this is what I do. My own followers will have no ease and comfort either, but I shall promote the cause of every sentient being by this form of life. Why think of life when you never know when death may come? If I wanted to I could have everything your Lama has of wealth and luxury, so why should I think of becoming one of his meanest followers? It is Buddhahood I am after and I am going all out to achieve it in this very lifetime. Look, Peta, you, too, give up these worldly aims of yours and come along with me, your elder brother, and pass your life in meditation in my new cave. If you could give up your worldliness you would find real happiness.'

And then I sang her a song devised on the spur of the moment, listing Lama Bari-Lotsa-wa's various possessions and claiming to be able to have them too, if I wished, but preferring to retire into the wilderness to meditate. The hour of death being so uncertain, no time must be wasted arguing. If she wished to cling to the world then she would build up an enormous karmic debt and if she saw the light then she could come with me to my mountain to meditate for the rest of the years at her disposal.

When my song was finished Peta shrugged: 'I see that you insist on identifying ease and comfort with worldliness. All these sermons of yours are only excuses because you know you can't ever become as well off as Lama Bari-Lotsa-wa. If I were to go to your mountain cave with you I should be utterly miserable with nothing to eat and nothing to wear —and I don't even know where Everest is. Now, please, brother, stay in one place and don't keep on rushing about here and there like an animal on the run, seeking shelter in caves and clinging to mountain ledges like a goat; then I could find you more easily. The people here seem to hold you in some veneration so it would be better to stay here perma-

nently. At any rate hold on for a few days. Make yourself a
garment with this blanket and I will come back again soon.'
And off she went to see what she could get by begging.

Dutifully I cut up the blanket and made first a cape to cover
my head, a little stall for each finger, a pair of coverings for
my feet and a stall for that whose presence had caused my
sister to blush so deeply! In a few days she came back and
demanded to see the results of my labour—and when I showed
her she was furious. One by one I put on each little cover. . . .

'You're utterly subhuman, brother,' she exclaimed, 'and
equally shameless; and, look, you've gone and spoilt the
blanket I took so much trouble to get for you. Sometimes
you seem to have no time to spare from your devotions and
at other times you can waste hours on a thing like this.'

'I assure you I am the most deserving of men,' I replied
equably, 'for I am turning my life to the best possible account.
Knowing what is really shameful and not falsely considered
so, I have taken up this religious life. You seemed to feel
ashamed of my natural shape, and as I could hardly afford to
cut off that which upsets you to look at so much, I made this
little stall for it; and as my other appendages were not dis-
similar I thought you would expect them to be covered
decently too. Your blanket isn't wasted; it's done what you
wanted for now I have a covering for my organ of shame.
As you are such a prude and more modest apparently than
myself, then let me tell you if I should feel ashamed how much
more so should you; you had better do away with your own
organs of shame quickly!' At this her face merely became
sulky, so I went on: 'People who are worldly see shame where
no shame is, but where there is something to be ashamed of,
like evil deeds, then they are not the least ashamed of themselves for doing them; so they have no real idea of what is
shameful and what not.' And then I sang her another song,

emphasising this point still more strongly and adding that ascetics who have given up the pleasures of the world and begun the Search for Truth do not need to conform to ordinary conventional standards of the modest and the immodest; my sister Peta was tormenting herself unnecessarily with all this.

She was still sulky, however, when I had finished and merely handed over the foodstuffs she had scraped together by begging, saying:

'You're obviously quite incorrigible and won't do anything I say, yet somehow I can't give you up. Take these and I'll see if I can get more,' and she turned to go; but, wishing to move her to my own way of thinking I managed to persuade her to stay for as long as the food held out so that even if she did not practise devotion, she would at least not be able to do anything she shouldn't while she was with me. While with me I expounded the doctrine of *Karma* to her incessantly and at last seemed to make a little impression, for she began to take a little more interest in religion than she had done.

And now who should arrive on the scene one day but that wicked old aunt of ours! It transpired that her husband having died, she had had a complete change of heart concerning her behaviour towards us and was filled with remorse for the wrongs the two of them had done, and now she had come with a yak-load of goods, looking everywhere for me. She had finally reached the village below my cave, where she had left the yak with its load and had climbed up the mountainside with whatever she could carry.

Peta saw her first and cried out to me: 'Why, here's that cruel aunt of ours who's the cause of all our troubles; don't let's have anything to do with her.' So saying she removed the tiny bridge across the chasm that separated my cave from the path on the other side.

130

Our aunt reached the cleft and stopped there, saying to Peta: 'Niece, don't take away the bridge; your old aunt is coming over.'

'That's why I'm taking it away,' Peta replied pertly.

'I can't blame you,' said Aunt, 'but I am truly most bitterly sorry for the things I have done to you both, so please put the bridge back again; or, if you won't, at least tell your brother I am here.'

It was at this moment that I arrived and sat down on a small knoll on our side. Aunt proceeded to make obeisance to me and pleaded with me to allow her to come over and talk. As a religious person I felt I should not refuse her request, which might be genuine, but that it would be as well to administer a few home truths first. So I said:

'I have renounced my relatives along with all worldly things and especially have I renounced you, Aunt, and my Uncle. Not satisfied with your persecution of us as children, when I had become an ascetic and chance led me to your door, you let loose the dogs on me and beat me cruelly.' Then I proceeded to sing to her of her misdeeds to a religious beggar, sparing no details in my description of her wickedness and ending by contrasting her behaviour with that of Peta, who had at least tried to help me materially despite her lack of interest in religion. And I adjured her to depart while the opportunity was there.

This all moved my aunt to tears and she admitted all my charges, but repeated her protestations of genuine repentance and begged my forgiveness. 'I have come from a real longing to see you,' she said. 'If you don't let me across to you I shall do away with myself.'

I could see that she was at last sincere and as it was my place to forgive when my pardon was asked under such circumstances, I began to put the bridge down, despite Peta at my elbow whispering that we shouldn't trust the old so-and-so an inch. However, her doubts were this time unfounded. Aunt really had had a change of heart and she came across to my cave with her offerings and sat down while I discoursed on *Karma* to her—so successfully, in fact, that she was converted and eventually developed herself to the uttermost in the religious life.

# X

# Milarepa on Karma

One of the other disciples now said: 'Master, we are struck
with admiration when we hear of your constancy and perseverance during your struggle to obtain the Truths from your
Guru and the perpetuation of that struggle to use what you
had received without regard to your bodily state, in lone-
liness and starvation. Beside yours our devotion seems to be
but child's play, on and off when we feel like it; by this sort of
devotion we shall never gain Deliverance as you have done.
Tell us what are we to do.'

'If you think of all the pain and troubles there are both in
this and in the lower world,' Milarepa replied, 'mine are not
all that bad either. Thoughtful people who have once heard
of the Doctrine of Karma and who believe in it, will find the
effort required. It is only those who hear the words and do not
grasp their significance who find themselves unable to give up
their attachments to the ways of the world. So you can see
how important belief in this doctrine is. Some people don't
admit even the most obvious incidents which are retributive,
to be due to Karma. They may go into advanced metaphysics
and talk about the Void as the Buddha taught it, without
realising that the Doctrine of the Void is far harder to comprehend than that of Karma. If one can truly grasp the idea of the
Void then the idea of Karma falls inevitably into place within
it, and then one has far more refined powers of perception with

regard to the quality of actions. Such a person becomes far more conscientious than other people.

'I started by accepting and understanding the Doctrine of Karma long before I grasped that of the Void; that's why I felt so deeply about evil I had done in my practice of Black Magic with the destruction of so many lives and so much property. I knew that, by Karmic Law, I would go down to the plane of Hell when I died. That's why I held so firmly to my Guru through thick and thin and persevered so rigorously in meditation. I had to. I would advise all you, my disciples, to practise meditation in solitude and asceticism, then you, too, will obtain Deliverance.'

Another of the disciples then broke out into a eulogy of our beloved Master, calling him Rimpoche (a title of the highest respect) and saying that he must have been a Buddha already before he was born because his life had been so devoted to religion, ready to sacrifice everything, even necessities for it. 'Ordinary mortals like us,' he went on, 'can't understand how you remained so humble and constantly faithful to your Guru after all you suffered at his hands. We couldn't think of undergoing so much hardship for the sake of our search for Truth; who could? And even were the spirit willing the flesh would be too weak. You surely must have been a Bodhisattva or a Buddha already; and how fortunate are we to have been associated with you now. We should certainly be able to obtain Deliverance just by that fact alone even if we do not work hard ourselves. Will you please tell us who you were in past lives?'

'I don't know for certain whose incarnation I am,' Milarepa replied, 'but even if I was born from one of the lowest planes, less than a human being almost, still your faith in me as something higher will stand you in good stead. Your personal love and regard for me make you think I am an Incarnation of some great person; but you sin against the Dharma by your doubts because you are not entirely sincere in your devotion. It is only by the great power of the Dharma that I am able to be where I am now, on the verge of Buddhahood despite the wickedness of my early youth. It was just because I firmly believed in Karma, or one's evil deeds rebounding on to oneself, that I pursued the Truth so zealously and unremittingly, and gave up all the attraction of this world.

'I was especially fortunate in being taken on by a perfected Guru who could give me just that which I needed most, the Truths best suited to me, which enabled me to follow the Short Path of the mystic Mantrayāna. He gave them to me without any unnecessary ritual or discourse, conferred on me the necessary Initiations and empowered me to meditate in the right way. It is certainly true that meditation on such truths would bring anyone else enlightenment in one lifetime. But a lifetime of crime also levies its own retribution. Without belief in this Law of Karma you lack incentive and zeal in devotion, whereas belief in it must surely spur you ever on to great efforts and the greater desire to obtain Buddhahood. Then your faith and humility in respect of the Guru, your zeal and meditational practice and finally your reaction to the experiences of your spiritual development will equal mine. And as soon as some spiritual development is attained people say, "Oh, he must have been born a Bodhisattva already!" and don't believe in the Short Path of the Mantrayāna.

'So my advice to you is to think about this Law of Karma, meditate on it, ponder on the biographies of other saints with their sufferings and troubles; think on the certainty of death and the uncertainty of the exact time of it; devote yourselves to study and practice. My spiritual knowledge has come through my renunciation of food, clothing and even name. Such was my enthusiasm that I bore every hardship, inured myself to every form of privation and went off to the most solitary places to meditate. Thus did I obtain knowledge and experience. Follow the same path and practise devotion as I have done.'

# XI

# Interlude

All this much of the narrative I am writing was told us by our beloved Guru himself; of what follows, some of it I was an eyewitness at and some of it I heard from other disciples who were with him until his death, or should one say, translation to Higher Planes? Yet when he had reached this point in his own history none of us was satisfied but we pressed him to tell us even more.

'Master,' I said, 'your tale at times is remarkably humorous and yet on the whole it is so pathetic that it all but brings tears to the eyes. Please tell us more of the funny bits.'

'The only true cause for laughter is in the story of my final success,' said the Guru, 'as the result of which I was enabled to save many beings and put them on the right path, both humans and beings on other Planes of existence, and so I served the Buddhist Faith.'

'Sir,' I asked further, 'who were your very first disciples, human or otherwise?'

'Non-human,' he replied, 'beings from a higher sphere first of all. Later human disciples began to gather.'

'Master,' said Seban, 'besides the hermitages you have mentioned where else have you practised your meditations?'

'There was another important place in Nepal,' Milarepa said, 'and in addition there were six outer well-known, six inner unknown and six secret caves; and yet another two, making twenty castles. There were, of course, also many small caves I inhabited from time to time wherever necessities appeared to be plentiful; until at last the object of meditation, the act of meditation and the meditator were so interwoven that now I do not know how to meditate.'

'Sir,' I said, as a thought occurred to me, 'we are basking in your reflected glory, benefiting from the fruits of your struggle and learning from you as you teach us; but it will not always be. Others will come who will have no opportunity for converse with you and who will never have known you, so, that they benefit from places where you yourself have been, please tell us the names of these caves so that they can visit them.'

Milarepa then named them all for our benefit and the benefit of those still to come. And deep was the faith developed in his hearers, at the account he had given us of his life story. We were all deeply touched by it and the more highly developed resolved to devote themselves wholly and entirely to following in his footsteps and to leave the world for a life of meditation. Many others, both men and women also who had been lay followers, now renewed their efforts and gave up their attachments to the things of the world and in time some of them became Yogis and Yoginis. Many of the less developed vowed to devote a certain amount of their daily time to the practice of meditation and others even lower in the spiritual scale, nevertheless determined to give up whatever might be an outstanding fault of theirs and to practise some particular good act in its place. So there was none who heard who did not improve and gain a little or much from hearing the narrative.

There is still much recorded that could be included here; the story of his struggle against non-human adversaries whom he managed in the end to convert; of the coming to him of his first disciples who were to be his closest followers and of others who came from time to time to hear the Dharma preached and to go away again the better for it. Much of this is in the form of song—Milarepa's own songs which he sang, as you know, whenever particularly moved or wanting to impress a point. Of these, perhaps the best known is the Song of the Snowfall, out of which he had emerged triumphant. Another also well known is the Hymn to the Pigeons.

There is also a chapter on record of how I myself first met my beloved Guru. At that time I was a leper—an outcast from society. But in a vision Milarepa saw me and was told that I should bring a certain Teaching from India to Tibet and he was told where to find me. And while he was meditating in a cave there I was directed to him and thereafter went back to India to be cured of my disease. At once I returned to my Master and lived with him in a cave where another disciple joined us. Other disciples he met in like manner, seemingly as if by chance. One of his pupils was a mere shepherd lad and many of them were women.

While in a cave at Nyanam along with some of his disciples, a great Indian Yogi named Dharma-Bodhi visited Milarepa and made obeisance to him. This was quickly spread around and increased the veneration and respect in which my Master was held there. But it also aroused the jealousy of another Lama who had a name for his metaphysical knowledge and debating prowess; he propounded some metaphysical questions to Milarepa, who easily answered them as the result of his Higher Powers. Shortly after this I went to India again and he knew telepathically of my return and came to meet me.

Many are the records of his meetings with various prominent persons who became his disciples, some of them ordained monks and already Gurus in their own right. Hardly anyone who came into contact with him failed to develop spiritually as a result.

So through his unbounded love for humanity Milarepa spread and strengthened the Buddhist Faith in the world of his day, saving many persons who would have been none the better for their lives had they not been with him.

## XII

# Attempted Murder

Now there was a learned Lama, named Tsaphuwa, with the title of Geshé, which denoted certain scholastic attainments of a high order; before the coming of Milarepa to Brin, he had held first place in the reverence and respect of the people of Brin. He pretended to esteem Milarepa very greatly, while at heart he was acutely jealous of him. He made a habit of putting difficult questions to him in public, ostensibly through desire for knowledge, but really to try and trip him up and make him look a fool; in which, of course, he was never successful.

Now that autumn Milarepa was invited to an important marriage feast, and he was given a seat above all the others. The Geshé was next below him, so, as was proper, the Geshé came and made obeisance before him, expecting Milarepa to rise and return it. But our Master had never made a practice of making obeisance to anyone except his Guru and he did not depart from this rule now. At this the Geshé was furious for he had admitted in public that he recognised Milarepa's superiority and he contrasted his rival's lack of academic distinction with his own name and fame and decided to show him up before all the guests.

With that he took a book from a fold in his robe and said: 'O Milarepa, please will you be so kind as to go through this book with me and explain some things I can't understand.'

But our Master was well aware of what was going on in the other's mind and answered:

'You are expert enough to know the meaning of this word by word, but to understand it fully—for that you have to eradicate the Eight Worldly Ambitions and to overcome your belief in your own personal ego, and to conquer yourself by solitary meditation. I have never studied the sophistry of the written word nor learned questions and answers by heart with which to discomfort my opponents; it only leads to mental confusion and is not the Way to Truth. Listen now!' And he sang of the means by which he had come to a realisation of the Unity of everything which annihilates the fallacious idea we all hold of 'I' and 'You', the subject–object relationship which does not exist in reality. 'Since my mind was filled with Truth it has sought no distraction,' he sang. 'By long contemplating Love and Compassion I forget there is a difference between myself and others; by meditating long upon my Guru I forget worldly power and prestige; meditating long upon my Guardian Deities I forget I am in a human body; meditating long on the Truths of Oral Transmission I have forgotten what is to be found in books; from long studying of True Science I have forgotten the knowledge that is based on Ignorance; from long contemplation of the Three Bodies I have forgotten how to hope or fear; long accustomed to solitary study I have forgotten how to ask advice from others; accustomed to apply my experience to my spiritual growth step by step, I have forgotten creeds and dogmas; from meditating long on the Absolute I have forgotten lesser objects; my mind being long truly Free, I have forgotten conventions and customs; long accustomed to humbleness of mind and body I have forgotten the ways of the proud and mighty; long accustomed to regard my body as my hermitage I have forgotten the ease and comfort of monastic life; long accustomed to know the meaning of the Wordless I have forgotten grammar and etymology: you, O learned one, may pursue this in ordinary standard works.'

The Geshé was unimpressed and said: 'That's all very well for a Yogi but such a religious theme shows no deep learning. I made obeisance to you thinking you were a very advanced doctor.'

This, however, roused the antagonism of the other guests, especially his own followers, and they rebuked him saying:

'Geshé, however learned you may be and however many more professors like you there may be in the whole world, all of you together are not equal to the smallest hair on Milarepa's body nor able to fill the pore from which it grows. You had better be satisfied with the seat you've been given which is above all the rest of us and go on making wealth by your practice of usury. As for religion, you are not in the least permeated with its perfume.'

This forthright statement angered the Lama still more but everyone being unanimously against him he had to retire into a sulky silence and thought to himself: 'Milarepa's an ignoramus; he just behaves eccentrically and invents things and so tends to overthrow the Buddhist Faith and swindles people by conjuring gifts out of them and I, who am the richest and most influential person in the whole district, count for less than a dog, despite my religious attainments. Something's going to be done about this!'

He picked, therefore, on one of his mistresses and promised her a turquoise if she would give Milarepa some poisoned curds to eat. She found him at his cave retreat and thereupon offered the dish of curds. But Milarepa could see easily into people and read their thoughts and he knew what she was about, even also that she had been bribed with a turquoise that she would not get until he had taken the curds. He knew further that he, himself, had almost completed his own life-work and would die shortly, poison or no poison. With all this clearly in mind he said to her:

'I won't take the food just now. Bring it again later and then I will eat it.'

The woman was frightened, thinking rightly that Milarepa might have been able to read her mind, so she returned to the Geshé and told him what had happened. She suggested that Milarepa, by clairvoyance, knew of the plot against him.

The Geshé, however, was not convinced that his rival had any such powers and he told his mistress so, urging that, had he known, he would have ordered her to eat the food herself, to prove her, and would not have told her merely to bring it again later. He then gave her the turquoise to encourage her and once more commanded her to take the food to Milarepa.

But the woman was afraid: 'They say that Milarepa does have this clairvoyant power,' she argued fearfully, 'and I am sure his refusal of the food proves it. He will certainly refuse it a second time. I don't want your jewel. I'm afraid to go again. I won't go.'

But the Geshé was not going to take 'No' for an answer: 'The common people believe it,' he said scornfully, 'but they are uneducated and easily duped by him. He's not like any clairvoyant person you will find described in the Scriptures, and I'm sure he's not. Look here, if you manage to get him to eat the food, seeing that you are already my mistress, I will take you as my proper wife; then it's not only one turquoise you will have but all my wealth will be for you to share. We have a common grudge against this fellow so make sure you're successful this time.'

The lure was sufficient to make the woman come once more to the Master and to offer him the dish of poisoned curds. With a smile Milarepa took it this time and remarked casually: 'You've got the turquoise all right for doing this!'

This was too much for the poor woman who fell down at his feet in fear and remorse and sobbed out the story, begging him not to take the poisoned food but to give it back that she might eat it and so atone for her crime.

'I can't possibly do that,' said Milarepa gently; 'I have too great compassion for you; if I did, it would be contrary to my Bodhisattva vows and that would spell disaster for me spiritually. It makes no odds; my life is finished anyway and it is time I left here for another world. Not that your poison would have any effect on me whatever. I only refused it first time to give you a chance to get the turquoise bribe. Now I shall take this food to satisfy the Geshé and to make sure he doesn't take it back from you again. But as regards the rest of his promises, don't rely on them at all, for you will be disappointed if you do. And don't believe a word of what he says about me. The time will come when both of you will rue this day. When that time comes plunge wholly into penance and devotion; and even if you can't do that, at least avoid such crimes even if your life is in jeopardy. Pray to me and my disciples in humble faith, because left to yourselves it would be many ages before you and your master were born into a happy life again. I will see what I can do to help you. But so long as I am alive keep this matter a secret; later, of course, everyone will know about it. You may not believe all I say but over this affair you will learn the truth of my words with respect to yourself. So bear it in mind and await developments.'

The woman returned and told the Geshé all this but he was still unimpressed and merely said: 'Everything spoken is not necessarily true. Enough that he has eaten the poison. Now we shall see. And mind you keep your mouth shut.'

Milarepa knowing that he must soon leave the world sent messages to all those who had known him and who had faith in him that they should visit him and bring a small offering with them. A similar invitation went out to numerous men and women who had never had an opportunity of meeting him before, and to all his disciples news was also sent, so that there was a mighty concourse of people from far and near, male and female, initiate and non-initiate, friends and strangers. And to them all Milarepa preached about Truth, Apparent and Real.

Many days were spent thus and those more spiritually gifted were able to see various psychic phenomena, such as another congregation of divine beings who listened eagerly in the sky above, and the joy of these spirits was communicated to the humans listening below. And to all and sundry minor phenomena such as rainbows, variegated clouds assuming odd shapes like panoplies and banners, were visible, and flowers fell down from the heavens and music was heard and fragrant odours permeated everywhere. The more highly developed who could see the celestial gathering asked the Guru how it was there was such a feeling of oneness between the heavenly presences and human beings and why the lesser signs that all could see had been manifested.

Milarepa replied: 'There are very few human beings who are spiritually developed, whether among the initiates or uninitiated, whereas the beings above, who are ever eager to hear the Dharma preached and are filled with joy whenever they do, are making offerings to me in worship. It is their joy which is radiated forth to all below and you can contact it and are aware of it.'

'Why can only so few of us see these Beings?' someone asked.

'If you are to see persons who have reached a state of de-

velopment whereby they are no longer born on Earth,'
Milarepa made answer, 'you yourself have to be endowed
with perfected vision; and that means not only devotional zeal
but freedom from the two basic fallacies of human thought:
belief in the Reality of what is only Phenomenal and belief
in the existence of the Ego. For this good deeds must out-
weigh all evil karma and then you can see yourself merged
into Pure Mind.' And with that he burst again into song to
make his point clear and help people to remember it, the
theme being the way by which one develops the power to see
the Higher Beings.

'Because of evil karma men, from the moment of their
birth almost, lapse into sin again and, worse still, delight in it
and so incur more bad karma. Yet evil karma can to some
extent be neutralised by the desire for goodness. But they
who sin deliberately sell their birthright for a mess of pottage.
Those with no clear idea of the Goal presume to act as guides
and teachers of others and so injure not only their pupils but
themselves as well. To avoid suffering oneself one must do
no harm to others. Repentance and confession at the feet of
one's Guru and a determination not to repeat one's offences is
the surest way to expiation. Sinners, however, for the most
part are clever, unstable of mind or purpose and are attached
to worldly pleasures, and they have no use for religion; which
shows they are swamped by their sins. So let each one of you
set about the process of expiation and then you, too, will see
the Higher Beings now thronging the heavens; and you will
also see, then, the true nature of your own mind and will
realise the identity of All, the Vision Infinite, the Round of
Birth and Death, and the State of Freedom. Then shall your
karma come to an end.'

This song had an effect to a lesser or greater extent on all
present according to the state of their development. Those

most highly evolved perceived the Truth in a sudden flash and won Emancipation there and then, and those less well evolved still experienced an Ecstatic Bliss they had never known before; and there was not one of the others who did not feel the desire for Deliverance for the first time in their lives.

Then Milarepa spoke again: 'All of you here to-day are here due to good karma you have collected in past lives and now, by being together, there is a certain pure and holy bond between us. I am old now and there is no guarantee that we shall meet again in this life so I implore you to remember my discourses and to put their teachings into practice in your daily lives to the best of your abilities. If you do, then in whatever realm I may arrive at the Perfection of Buddhahood you shall be the first to receive the Truth I shall teach. Take comfort in this thought.'

Now when the people from Nyanam heard this they asked the Guru if he would come to their country to die there, or at least to pay it a final visit; the men of Tingri did the same. But Milarepa replied that he was too old to go travelling any more, and that he would die in the land he was now dwelling in. 'So make your farewells now and go to your own homes and we shall meet again hereafter,' he said.

They then asked that he would bless their respective countries and each place he had ever visited, making a special good wish for everyone he had ever met and who had listened to his preaching; in short upon all sentient creatures.

'I am grateful to you for your faith in me,' Milarepa replied, 'and also for the way you have kept me supplied with the necessities of life. I, on my part, have shown what I feel about you by having preached to you and wished you well, so that a bond has been forged between us. And now seeing that I am a Yogi who has obtained Enlightenment it is my duty to give you my blessing and good wishes for your welfare, spiritual and material.' With that he sang a short hymn of gratitude and blessing expressing the hope that all those who might hear or read of his life would be moved to emulate it and that Deliverance might at last come to every form of life down to the smallest insect.

The great gathering now dispersed much comforted but the people of Brin asked Milarepa if he would go on preaching to them; and this he did for some time. One day he said:

'Anyone with any questions or problems to be elucidated should present them quickly for I have not much more time to live.'

A special *puja* was then made and all difficulties were cleared up. Afterwards two of his closest disciples came to him and said: 'Sir, from what you have said we are afraid you intend to die. Surely your life cannot be finished yet?'

The Master answered them: 'Both my life and my influence for converting others is finished. Now therefore, since I was born, I must die.'

A few days later he seemed to be ill and at once a leading pupil began to make preparations for interceding on his behalf with the Powers that be and begged his Guru to take medical treatment also. But Milarepa replied that illness in a Yogi should be a spur to drive him on and prayers should not be offered for his recovery; he should use his illness to progress spiritually and ever be ready for suffering and even death. But he himself, through Marpa's teaching, knew all the methods for overcoming illness in himself and he needed no interceders. 'The time has come,' he said, 'when the body that is mind-evolved only must become merged into the Realm of Light and no rites are necessary for this. Worldly people who have heaped up a bad karma for themselves by wrong-doing naturally try to put off the day of their death by drugs and sacrifices and prayers. Yet there is no means by which anyone can postpone the decreed Day of his Death. If there are any fearful because of this who really want to attain eternal bliss I know the secret of it.'

The disciples who heard naturally at once demanded that he should disclose the secret to them and Milarepa told them: 'All worldly pursuits have but one inevitable result: sorrow. Gains end in losses, buildings in destruction, meetings in partings, birth ends in death. Knowing this one should right from the start abandon ideas of collecting things, of building or of meetings. Find a Guru and, obeying him implicitly, set about the realisation of Truth which transcends birth and death.'

His two closest disciples then suggested that if he could recover and live a little longer there would be many more beings to whom he could do good. And so they asked that he would perform a Tantric rite to prolong his life and also to take some medicine.

'My time has come,' returned the Master, 'otherwise I might have done so. But remember, anyone performing Tantric rites to prolong life except for the purpose of serving others, would be behaving most improperly towards the deities and it would have a karmic reaction. Never, never perform Tantric rites for personal gain or for worldly ends. Most of my life I have been practising Higher Tantric Rites and these keep me firm now. Moreover Marpa's remedies for the eradication of the Five Poisons of lust, hatred, stupidity, egotism and jealousy, serve as my medicines. But you, now, it is not sufficient for you merely to be devotees or to have adopted a religious life, you must also use Trouble and Adversity as aids along the Path. If one's time is not yet come there is no harm in seeing a doctor and letting him treat one —even the Buddha himself allowed his Physician, Jivaka

Kumara, to feel his pulse and prescribe for him, but when his time was come he used nothing to ward it off but passed away into his Parinirvana. So now my time has come and I, too, will do nothing to prevent it.'

Accepting the inevitable at last the disciples then asked for instructions as regards funeral arrangements, relics of his bones and articles and the raising of *stupas*; also who was to be his successor and what ceremonies were to record the anniversary of his death; and what was the correct line of meditation for each disciple respectively.

Milarepa replied: 'Due to Marpa I have obtained Deliverance from the world of illusion. There is no guarantee that my body will remain after my death. So there is no need of stupas or memorials of any sort. As I own no monastery I have no need of appointing a successor. Anyone may possess and dwell in my caves and mountain peaks and other solitary hermitages. Instead of erecting *stupas* cultivate a loving devotion to all parts of the Dharma and set up the Banner of Love, and in place of memorials let there be daily prayers. For anniversaries make extra offerings of prayers. For your own practice, if you find a certain habit helpful, cultivate it, even if it contravenes convention, provided it tends to counteract the Five Evil Passions; if harmful and distractive, abandon it even if it is generally approved. Anyone who fails to follow my advice, however learned he may be, will sink deep down into Hell. Life is short, the moment of death unknown to you, so apply yourselves to meditation. Avoid doing evil even if it costs you your life. As a universal rule: Act so that you have no cause to be ashamed of yourselves. Abide by this rule. Then you can be certain you will be following the commands of all the Buddhas there have ever been. And then I, too, will be satisfied. Nothing else will satisfy this old heart of mine.' Milarepa then chanted a hymn to amplify the points he had made. 'If you do as I have commanded then shall not only I but all the Buddhas be well content. What is the value of an Initiation if one's Guru is not in an unbroken line of apostolic succession. Unless one blends the Dharma with one's own nature what is the use of being able to recite Tantras by heart? Unless one has renounced worldly things what is the use of meditation? Unless one practises the Doctrine in one's whole life, what is the use of performing religious ceremonies and rites? Unless one conquers anger by love what is the good of meditating on patience? Unless one is free from likes and dislikes, what is the point of worshipping? Unless all selfishness is overcome what is the use of giving alms? Unless one is filled with pure love and veneration what is the use of building a *stupa*? Unless prayer comes from the depths of the heart what is the use of celebrating anniversaries? Unless the Secret Teaching is kept in mind what profit comes of suffering? Unless you have loved and trusted implicitly a Saint when living, what is the use of contemplating his relics? Unless one feels repentance in oneself, what is the use of saying: 'Repent!' Unless one meditates on loving others more than oneself what is the use of exclamations of pity? Unless one has overcome attachments what is the use of rendering service only when one feels like it? Unless the Guru's word is always held in regard and obeyed implicitly, what is the point of having many disciples? Any actions which are not of positive value merely do you harm, so refrain from them. The Yogi who has carried out his own mission has no need to shoulder other responsibilities.' Thus sang Milarepa and impressed his hearers with his wisdom.

It now became obvious that the Master was sick and when he heard of it, the Geshé who had tried to poison him unsuccessfully came to see him with a small offering of meat and beer and addressed him in the most unctuous of tones:

'Such a saintly person as Jetsun Milarepa,' he he said silkily, 'really should not be seriously ill. But since he obviously is, his sickness should be distributed among his disciples. Or, if it can be transferred, how about transferring it to someone like myself? But of course you couldn't possibly do that, so what's to be done?'

Milarepa smiled and made a soft answer: 'There was really no need for me to have had this illness, but I had no choice in the matter as perhaps you know. Normally, a Yogi's illness is different from that of an ordinary person although it may still seem to be accidental. But this illness, in my case, is of benefit. I could transfer if there was any point in doing so, but there isn't.'

The Geshé thought to himself that Milarepa suspected him of having tried to poison him but had no proof; he certainly did not believe Milarepa had the power to transfer the illness, so he decided to goad him still further:

'Oh, Jetsun,' he said, 'I wish I knew the cause of your illness. If it is caused by malignant spirits they should be exorcised. If it is just a stomach upset this should be put right. But I don't know what is supposed to be the matter with you. If you are able to transfer it, please do transfer it to me.'

'A certain person,' Milarepa replied, 'became obsessed by an evil spirit indeed, the Demon of Egotism. This was the cause of my illness. This Demon cannot be exorcised, neither can the disease be cured. If I were to transfer it to you you would not be able to endure it for even one minute. So I shall not transfer it.'

'Hah,' thought the Geshé to himself again, 'he is not prepared to admit he hasn't the power to transfer it; he's just pretending he doesn't want to.' So he said again:

'Please, I beg you to transfer it!'

'Very well,' said Milarepa, 'I will transfer it, not to you, but to that door over there, and you can see the force of it.'

At once the door began to creak and groan; it throbbed and vibrated and it seemed as if the wood would split. And for that period the Guru seemed to be free of pain himself.

'This is just illusion, a form of hypnosis,' thought the Geshé, so he said out loud: 'Wonderful. Now do please transfer it to me.'

'All right, since you insist, I will show what just a little of the pain is like,' Milarepa answered. He took back the disrupting force from the door, gave but one half of it to the Geshé and asked him whether he thought even that much pain bearable.

Then the Geshé was in such dreadful agony that he almost fainted, and as the result of having felt only a half of the pain he had caused Milarepa, he was filled with true repentance and bowing down before him, his head on Jetsun's feet, he cried: 'O Divine Master, as you say this illness was caused by a worthless, selfish, jealous creature; I beg that you will accept all my worldly goods and property and forgive me my crime that the evil karma may not swamp me.'

His remorse was obviously sincere enough and Milarepa readily forgave him. He took back the whole of the pain and said: 'All my life I have never owned house or property, and now on my deathbed when I have no need whatsoever of possessions, what should I do with your worldly goods? Keep them yourself and in future refrain from sinning against the Precepts of the Dharma. I will do what I can for you as regards your present situation that you may not suffer for your wrongdoing.'

And he chanted a hymn showing his great compassion for humanity which gave the Geshé some measure of comfort.

There and then, in religious zeal, he vowed to devote himself
to the good life and to shun all evil deeds, which deeds, he
told Jetsun, were due to his love of wealth and property.
'Henceforth I want no lands or houses,' he affirmed, 'so even
if you do not need my possessions perhaps they will be of
use to assist in maintaining your disciples and followers. Please
do accept them.'

Despite this earnest sincerity, however, Milarepa maintained his refusal, but after his death the disciples accepted
them to defray the funeral expenses and to pay the cost of
festivals commemorating his passing away. And the Geshé
himself became a devotee in the end.

'As a reward for my staying on here,' commented our
Master, 'a hardened sinner has been converted. Now there is
no further need for a Yogi to remain in this worldly prison.
Yet a Yogi should not die in a village such as this. I will go
to a big town; I will go to Chubar.'

'It will be much too tiring in your present state of health, if
you walk,' said Seban-Repa, one of his disciples; 'we will
carry you in a sedan chair, Sir.'

'There is no reality either in health or illness,' Milarepa replied. 'Here I have manifested the phenomenon of illness. At
Chubar I shall manifest the phenomenon of death. Some of
my younger disciples may go on ahead to Chubar to make
things ready.'

And now there occurred a seeming miracle, for not one but
many Milarepas went to Chubar, in different company and
by different routes. When the young disciples who had been
sent on ahead arrived at their destination they found their
Master already there; yet he was also with others on the road,
and at the same time lying ill elsewhere. Yet another of his
forms was preaching a sermon at Red Rock, and to all those
who had had to remain at home and who were making an

offering on his behalf, did he also show himself. You can imagine what heated discussion there was, therefore, among the disciples when they all met together at Chubar, each saying that their beloved Master had been with them and so could not have been with the others who also claimed him.

So heated did it become, indeed, that finally they came to Milarepa in a body and demanded to be told the truth about this extraordinary state of affairs.

'You are all right. I was just having some fun with you,' said the Guru casually. And with that they had to be satisfied.

He now took up residence at Chubar and his illness increased. Natural phenomena also accompanied his sermons and the whole countryside was suffused with a supernatural glory. Then two of his leading disciples asked him to what realm he was going and where they should address their prayers to him. They further asked if he had final instructions to give and begged him to give them each special guidance as to the best line for his devotional practice.

'Direct your prayers wherever you feel it best,' Milarepa told them; 'wherever you pray, as long as you are sincere and in earnest, I shall be there with you. So pray earnestly and unwavering. I am going to the Realm of Happiness first of all. Now my last will and testimony is as follows:

'To Rechung, who will soon arrive' (as I said before, I regrettably had been absent all this time) 'give my bamboo staff and this cotton cloth which you see are my sole personal possessions. They will act as a talisman to help him in the Control of Vital Airs. Until Rechung arrives no one is to touch my body. Upa-Tonpa is to have the Hat of the Master Maitri and this black staff, which will carry with them success in deep meditation and high aspiration for upholding the Faith. Shiwa-Wod is to have the wooden bowl. The skullcap I give to Ngan. To you, Seban-Repa, I leave my flint

and steel. This bone spoon BriGom may have. For the rest
of the disciples, this cotton mantle can be divided up in strips.
These things are of no value materially but they all carry with
them my blessing.'

He then went on to say something that surprised his hearers
very much: 'Now for the main part of my will which none
but my chief disciples and lay followers should be told of:
All the gold that I, Milarepa, have amassed in my lifetime is
hidden beneath this hearth, and with it there are instructions
as to how it is to be distributed among you all. When I am
gone don't fail to look for it and obey the instructions you
find.

'With regard to the carrying out of my religious teachings
in your everyday lives, just remember this: There are some
among you who take pride in outward shows of sanctity but
who inwardly are concerned only with the name and fame
they can acquire thereby. Without caring that this is not only
valueless but actually harmful, they persevere in it purely
from selfishness. Such hypocrisy, the clinging to the pleasures
of the world while appearing to be devout, is like taking the
richest and most delicious of food well soaked with poison.
So drink not of this poison of desire for wordly fame but cast
off the shackles of doing 'good works' which only lead to
more desire for the reputation of being one who does 'good
works', and practise earnest and sincere devotion.'

On being asked whether it was permissible to carry out
worldly duties to a small extent for the benefit of others
Milarepa replied:

'Yes, provided there is absolutely no trace of self-interest in
so doing. But remember, true altruistic detachment is very
rare and "good works" seldom have the right effect unless they
are purely altruistic. It is as if one drowning man tried to save
another drowning man. One should not be over hasty in

setting out to help others before one has realised the Truth; if one does it is a case of the blind leading the blind. So long as the sky is above you, there will be no end to the sentient beings who need help, so everyone has an opportunity to serve when he is ready. Until the opportunity shows, however, I do impress on you the need to stick to the one resolve only: the attainment of Buddhahood for the good of all beings. Be meek and unpretentious. Dress in rags. Care nothing for hardship with respect to food and dress. Renounce all thought of worldly fame. Use adversities of mind and body as penances and so learn from them. And remember my words so that your study and your practice in adversity follows the right Way.'

With the need to drive his point home once and for all, Milarepa then sang to his two disciples, that they might remember his words the better:

'If you would be true devotees look not for worldly reputation in your Guru, for little will come of the association. If you do not have the Initiation, the words of the Tantras will merely become additional fetters. If you do not live by the Tantric Scriptures all practice of the rites will but ensnare you the more deeply. If you do not meditate on the Teachings, mere world renunciation will give you little benefit. If you do not subdue evil passions by Love, mere preaching will be but empty sounds. If you do not follow the subtle Methods, mere perseverance will yield but little gain. If you do not know the Secret the Path for your zeal will be long indeed. If you do not work for your own Deliverance you will remain bound to the Wheel of Birth and Death. If you are not prepared to give up all your worldly possessions in the Search for Truth, much meditation will profit you little. If you are not content in yourselves, whatever you have will only benefit others. If you have not Peace within you, the pleasures and comforts of the body will become a source of pain. If you do not suppress Ambition, desire for fame will lead to ruin and litigation. Sycophancy stimulates the lower natures of men, the desire for gain drives a wedge between friends. If you do not answer back you will not find yourself in a court of law; retain perfect equanimity and your mind will be concentrated. Dwell alone and you will find a friend! Take the lowest seat and you will find yourself raised to a higher. Hasten slowly and you will arrive the sooner. Renounce all worldly aims and you will achieve the Highest Goal. If you tread the Secret Path, you will find the shortest way. If you comprehend the Void, you will find yourself developing Compassion. If you give up the idea of yourself versus the rest of the world, you will become fit to offer your services to it. And when you are successful in serving others, then you and I will meet again; and when you find me you will attain Buddhahood. Pray to me, and to the Buddha and to the Sangha without distinguishing between the three.'

This was the theme of Milarepa's song. He then added the words: 'Since I may not live much longer, take heed of my Teaching and follow me.' And with that he seemed to sink into a trance from which he never awoke. And so he died in his eighty-fourth year, in the last month of the Wood-Hare year (January, A.D. 1135).

# XIII

# Death of Milarepa—and After

If there had been phenomena seen during his last days, at the passing of the Great Guru these were redoubled. Beauty was the keynote; beauty in appearance, beauty in sounds and beauty in odours; and hymns of praise filled the air. Spirits from Higher Planes became visible to mortal men, bearing offerings and paying their last respects to the departed Saint, and, strangest of all, these spirits entered into communication with the men of the earth who also worshipped the Master.

The people of Nyanam, a nearby town, when they heard of the death of Milarepa asked the disciples for the privilege of disposing of the body in their town. But this request was refused. Then they asked that cremation should be postponed until they had time to go to Brin for all of his followers who were still there. This was granted, but when they returned it was with a strong body of men, intending to take away the remains of the Guru by force. It seemed as if there would be a violent scene and the disciples tried to intervene and calm tempers by saying, 'Look here, men of Nyanam and Brin! You all believed in Jetsun Milarepa and were his followers. Seeing that he died in Chubar it is only right that he should be cremated here. Stay, then, until the cremation is over and you will be given your share of the ashes and relics.' But the people of Nyanam, thinking they were sufficiently strong, were about to remove the corpse forcibly when a god appeared in the sky and in the voice of Milarepa himself, sang to them a hymn telling them how stupid it was to fight over a mere body; nor was that the way to get it, but if they remained faithful and prayed there would be enough relics for all.

The voice of their beloved Master, heard again, had a quietening effect on all his followers and they paid heed to his words and turned from thoughts of violence to prayer. By a miracle the people of Brin and of Nyanam found they each seemed to have a corpse of Jetsun to themselves, while the real corpse lay at Chubar. So, well satisfied, each performed their own cremation ceremony in their own town.

The leading disciples were, of course, at Chubar and they prayed day and night beside the bier while the body seemed to measure less and less and emitted a radiant halo. When it was no larger than that of an eight-year-old child, the disciples, who had been waiting for my coming, as the Master had bidden them, now said to each other:

'It doesn't look as if Rechung is coming at all. If we wait much longer there won't be anything left to cremate and then we shall have no relics to worship. It would be best to proceed with the cremation at once.'

This was unanimously agreed upon so the body was carried in state to a great boulder from which our Guru had often preached. On this the funeral pyre was built, and everyone paid their last respects to it. But no amount of kindling would set the pyre alight. After repeated efforts had failed a group of five spirits appeared in the sky and sang to the dejected disciples, who gazed up at them in wonder.

'*Rom!*\* The divine fire of the Vital Force has ever been

---

\* Or *Rang*, the *Bya* (or 'Seed') Mantra of the Element Fire.

contemplated by him. What power has fire over such a one? When one has spent his life in meditation, what need is there of leaving a body behind? He is above all your funeral arrangements and can well dispense with them. The very heavens are celebrating, what need is there of your rites? The mortal remains of he who has become Enlightened has no need of conventional rituals. Rather, therefore, worship and pray; speak not of "my" and "your" with respect to his corpse. Keep silent about the secret Teachings; seek solitude; you will reap your reward from the death of your Master, never fear! Give heed to Jetsun's final instructions and do not contravene them, and a blessing on you all.'

This was in effect what they sang and Ngan-Dzong said: 'This confirms our Master's command that we do not cremate his body before Rechung arrives. But there is no guarantee that he will come and the body is fast disappearing and will do so altogether if we put off its cremation and then there will be no relics.'

Shiwa-Wod-Repa then said: 'Milarepa's own orders, the spirits' song and the fact that the pyre won't light all point to the same thing. Rechung is sure to arrive soon. So let's keep on praying.' And this they did.

Now at this time I was staying at a certain monastery some distance away and one night I had a vision in which I saw a cenotaph being worshipped by men and by spirits and many of my Master's disciples were around it. Then from the cenotaph I thought I saw my beloved Guru himself lean out and speak to me saying how glad he was to see me again, and we conversed together and he stroked my hair; I felt all my great love for him go forth, and then I awoke.

My first thought was: 'Can my Guru have died?' and this thought was accompanied by a great longing to see my Master again so that I set out to seek him. As I started a spirit seemed to say to me: 'Rechung, hurry, for unless you do you will not see your Guru alive. Go at once.'

This urged me on to still greater effort and by the exercise of mental control and special breathing by dawn I had accomplished a full two months' donkey journey in the space of a few hours. Pausing on a mountain peak for rest, I had another vision of a great gathering of the gods and Higher Beings all going in the same direction and carrying offerings. I asked of them where they were going for my heart was gripped by fear.

'Have you been blind and deaf to recent events?' one answered, 'that you don't know what has been happening? All these signs in the heavens mark the passing to Holier Realms of Jetsun Milarepa, so all who honour the Dharma are come to worship him, while mortals are gathered at Chubar for the same purpose.'

I felt as if my heart would break when I heard this and hurried on at full speed and as I neared Chubar, there I saw my Guru seated on a boulder. He greeted me warmly and stroked my head just as he had done in my vision and I was overjoyed that he was not dead after all and made profound obeisance to him. Then I asked him many questions to which he replied and finally he said:

'My son, Rechung, you take your time about coming; I will go ahead to make things ready for you,' and with that he departed out of sight.

Now when I got to Chubar, of course, there was no sign of him, but around the cave where he had lived were many disciples and lay followers mourning and worshipping, and at once I realised what had happened.

Unfortunately some of the disciples who were fairly new did not know me and they refused to let me go near the body of their Master and mine. At this I was deeply grieved and sang a hymn to my Guru expressing the agony of spirit I felt. I began by a paeon of worship and then appealing to him on the grounds that I had been his favourite disciple I besought him to allow me to see his face just once again and to hear his voice so full of Wisdom and Divine Instruction. Unworthy though I was, I prayed that he might have compassion on me.

As soon as I had sung this hymn with all the feeling of a broken heart, the colour of Milarepa's corpse, which had faded, suddenly became brilliant and the pyre took fire so that the wood blazed merrily. At the same time, Shiwa-Wod, Ngan-Dzong and Seban-Repan, some of my contemporaries, came to welcome me, but I still smarted under my rejection by the other younger followers.

Now so great was my faith and sincerity that it seemed as if it reanimated the corpse, which sat up amid the flames and spoke thus:

'Oh, you younger disciples, don't behave like this. One lion is far preferable to a hundred tigers. And such a lion is my son Rechung. Allow him to approach. And you, my son, Rechung, do not feel so deeply about it but come near to your Father.'

Everybody was startled at this, as well may be imagined, and then they were overwhelmed with joy and I leaped forward and touched my beloved Guru with tears pouring down my cheeks and so overcome was I that I fainted clean away. When I came to there were all the disciples seated around the pyre, while Jetsun Milarepa had risen in the Body of Spirit and was to be seen seated entire among the flames which seemed to enthrone like a lotus flower, and with one knee bent and his right hand extended in his favourite preaching attitude, he spoke:

'Listen to the last words of an old man and to my final

Teaching. Rechung, my son, most dear to me, hear this hymn and heed my precepts: Beware of the physical body which is a culprit indeed, in ceaseless craving for its food and dress it can find no refuge from worldly worries. In the mental world the culprit is the phenomenal mind which, the slave of the body, has no time to realise the true nature of the Mind nor to comprehend Reality. On the frontier of Intelligence and Matter, the culprit is knowledge from experience of the senses, ever on its guard against its own downfall; it has no time to discover the nature of Truth. Rechung, keep to uncreated Knowledge. Upon the frontier of this and the future life the culprit is consciousness, imagining itself to be other and greater than it is and finds no time to realise the Truth. Rechung, find the nature of Eternal Truth. In the world of Illusion the culprit is the sin productive of Karma from which arise desire and attachment. Rechung, avoid likes and dislikes. Many subtle and apparent truths are there, dealing with which one finds no time for real Truth. Rechung, avoid subtle argument. Gurus and Higher Beings, combine these in a single whole and worship that. Your aim, meditation and practice, combine these to win Knowledge. Think of past, future and the present all as one and accustom yourself to the idea. This is my last Testament, Rechung, my son; beyond this there is no more Truth. Learn from it.'

The flames now blazed the higher and assumed the shape of a square mansion with four entrances and ornamentation, enhaloed by a rainbow and curtains of light. It seemed as if roofs and domes were there in the fire, and at the base the flames curled themselves like the petals of a giant lotus flower. The crackling of the wood was as the music of different instruments. The smoke smelled like the most fragrant incense. Above the funeral pyre the sky was filled with spirits and Higher Beings; some brought nectar which they poured down, others food and drink, unguents and perfumes of which the humans below were able to partake. Then the female spirits chanted a farewell hymn to our Master:

'Because their Lord is gone from them some are weeping in their grief, some have even lost consciousness from the depth of their emotion. Yet with all this mourning, did not the flames burst forth unkindled and assume wondrous and symbolic shapes? Was not the sound of the crackling like the music of cymbals and conch-shells, harps, flutes and drums? And from the very sparks did not forms of goddesses seem to spring? These goddesses have borne away from the funeral pyre the charred bones and ashes of him who has surrendered his earthly vehicle. He has assumed the Body of Truth which permeates all from which human and other beings can draw benefit.

'That which is by nature Uncreate, Unborn, the Void, that has no beginning and no end, that is the Real Truth.'

By this time it was evening and the fire had burnt itself out. Now another miracle appeared. For the cremation-house was empty so it seemed, yet some disciples saw it in a great cenotaph, others saw manifestations of past Buddhas, others saw various religious symbols, others a mass of blazing gold, others a pool of clear water and yet others saw nothing at all.

They then opened the doors of the cremation-house that the ashes might cool and we went to sleep that night dreaming of the relics that would be ours on the morrow. I myself had a dream that some female Spirits were taking a sphere of Light from the cremation-house and I watched them fascinated. Then it suddenly occurred to me that they might be taking away the ashes and the relics and I awoke in a fright and dashed into the cremation-house with some of my companions. The ashes and bones had all been swept away! Not a particle of dust, not an ash was on the floor. In acute distress I prayed to the Female Spirits of my dream and demanded that they return the relics and the ashes for the benefit of human beings.

Came the reply from the spirit world: 'You, the chief disciples, have you not all obtained the best relics you can ever have, the Truths by which you have the Dharma formed in your own minds. If that is not enough, pray then to your Master and perhaps he will grant you something. And what has the rest of mankind done to deserve any relics? It has not even appreciated Milarepa when he was on earth, despite his being so lofty a Being. No, they deserve no relics at all. These belong to us.'

We disciples realised that the Spirits were speaking the truth, so we prayed to our Guru that he should, after all, allow us some of his relics, reminding him of his own hard life and the little part we had played in it. How kind he had been to us then, could he now prove less kind and understanding?

When we had sung thus there came down from the Realm of Light an orb as large as an egg and from it was emitted a ray. Each of us stretched out our hands to seize it for himself but it rose again out of reach and was taken up to the heavens. In its place appeared a great Cenotaph inside which was an image of Milarepa; two Female Spirits guarded it, one on either side, and sang yet another hymn:

'Sons and disciples: you have called on the name of your spiritual Father and prayed for a relic. This orb which you have seen was a manifestation of the Body of Truth itself. How could it belong to any single one of you? It is not private property to be clutched at thus! To you has now been granted to see strange sights and symbols. The Guru, embodied in the Truth, manifests Himself in every conceivable form by super-normal power. Cling to your Faith in him. If you separate yourselves from the world you will become surrounded by the Higher Beings: if your religious practices are sincere you will achieve success in Yoga: if you are content with your own situation it will be clear that your evil passions are uprooted: if you cling not to self and possessions, it will be clear that your desires are under control: if you heed not differences in caste or creed you will hold a Right Viewpoint: if you see the identity of Nirvana and this world with the Void, your Meditation will be Right. If you have zeal and energy your Acts will be Right: If Guru and chela are united in their hearts, then will their relationship be Right. If you receive good omens of success and divine gifts, then your Thoughts will be Right. So, let Good Faith and Mutual Experience and Satisfaction be your Relics.'

The cenotaph was still in full view as the Spirits held it aloft above our heads. As they showed signs of departing with it, however, my friend and brother disciple, Shiwa-Wod-Repa, added a final entreaty in his fine musical voice and they stayed to listen:

'Oh, Father, you who were incarnate to help humanity, Divine Yogi, who now pervade the All as Truth itself, to you we pray that you will grant to us, your chelas, this cenotaph the Spirits now hold. Lord, when on earth you met with other Yogis you shone amongst them, a Master of the Ascetic life; to you we pray: grant to us, your chelas, this cenotaph the Spirits hold. Lord, when you served your Guru, so meek and patient were you, ready to do the most menial task; to you we pray: grant to us, your chelas, this cenotaph the Spirits hold. Lord, when you renounced all worldly aims you were Master of the Masters, a Yogi resolute, of mighty courage; to you we pray: grant to us, your chelas, the cenotaph the spirits hold. Lord, when meditating on your Guru's Teaching you were as a tigress feeding on the flesh of men, undoubting, unswerving, ever persevering: grant to us, your chelas, the cenotaph the spirits hold. Lord, when you were passing through the wilderness like iron granite were you in determination, a Yogi unchanging; to you we pray: grant to us, your chelas, this cenotaph the spirits hold. Lord, when you began to reach Enlightenment and showed the signs of super-human Powers, you remained strong and fearless; to you we pray: grant to us, your chelas, the cenotaph the spirits hold. Lord, when you gained the Power of generating Vital Heat, your own Light spread over the world; to you who has all craving lost we pray: grant to us, your chelas, the cenotaph the spirits hold. Lord, when you and your chelas met, it was like the sun striking upon the fire-glass and you made us Masters of our minds; to you we pray: grant to us, your chelas, the cenotaph the spirits hold. Lord, when one would have given you his worldly goods you remained unsullied by any greed; to you we pray: grant to us, your chelas, the cenotaph the spirits hold. Lord, when you used to preach to many thousands, like the sun over the dull world were you; to you, the Wise and Loving One we pray: grant to us, your chelas, this cenotaph the spirits hold. Lord when you were here on earth and people saw you, it was like a mother meeting her son, all things for their good you did; to you we pray: grant to us, your chelas, the cenotaph the spirits hold. Lord, when you are departing to the Realms of Light, you are like a treasure chest of blessings; to you we pray: grant to us, your chelas, the cenotaph the spirits hold. Lord, when you prophesied you were always right. Knower of the past, the present and the future, to you we pray: grant to us, your chelas, the cenotaph the spirits hold. Lord, when you granted a boon it was like a father giving to his son, nothing did you hold back. To you we pray: grant to us, your chelas, the cenotaph the spirits hold.'

He finished his hymn and then we heard the voice of our beloved Guru coming from the cenotaph poised above us in answer, with a last sermon for our instruction.

'You who, with faith and much promise of a great future, pray to me, listen now while I expound to you, cotton-clad disciple of mine. Of the Body of Truth which I have realised, none may say "It is mine" or "I have it" or "I have it not". It is of the nature of the Void. The orb you saw was what remained of my earthly body and now it has become this cenotaph you are beholding. In the Divine Realm it will remain for ever, attended by Spirits who, with other Higher Beings, will worship it. If given to human beings it would slowly disintegrate. You my spiritual sons and followers have had your share of relics in the Knowledge I have given you so that you, too, may realise the Body of Truth in your own minds. Think now upon those Similarities which, if confused, will lead to error. The serving of a perfect Guru and the serving of a prosperous person are alike, yet not alike. Confuse them not. The true comprehension of the Void in one's mind and illusory obsessions of consciousness are alike, yet not alike. Confuse them not. The knowing of the Pure State by Meditation and fondness for the tranquillity born of the ecstatic trance of Quiescence are alike, yet not alike. Confuse them not. The Flood of Deep Intuition and other deep convictions of what is right and true are alike, yet not alike. Confuse them not. The clear perception of the concentrated Mind and the noble impulse to serve others are alike, yet not alike. Confuse them not. Spiritual harvest and worldly prosperity brought are alike, yet not alike. Confuse them not. Spiritual guidance and commands from Higher Sources, and the temptations of lower elements are alike, yet not alike. Confuse them not. The Orb of the Body of Truth and a man-made orb are alike, yet not alike. Confuse them not. The true Nirvana and the Heavenly Blossom of a Sensual Paradise are alike, yet not alike. Confuse them not. A cenotaph made by the gods and one made by devils are alike, yet not alike. Confuse them not. The faith borne of past good karmas and that produced by accident are alike, yet not alike. Confuse them not. True faith from the depths of the heart spontane-ously arising and faith of convention and upbringing are alike, yet not alike. Confuse them not. Sincere devotion to study of the Dharma and pretended devotion to please the Guru are alike, yet not alike. Confuse them not. True success realised and reputation for success are alike, yet not alike. Confuse them not.

'This cenotaph symbolises the Buddhas of the Past, the Buddhas of the Present and the Buddhas of the Future. Here they meet. Here, too, your Guru Milarepa meditates. It will be borne now to the Realm of Happiness where a ready welcome will be accorded it. If to this cenotaph you pray with sincerity and devotion and to it make offerings in venera-tion, you will be protected within your own immutable Faith, and if you long for the power of Individual Wisdom, beneath the cenotaph bow your heads.'

We could now see the monument being carried through the sky and as it passed over our heads rays of light fell from it striking the heads of every one of the disciples there assem-bled. We had a vision of some of the Highest Deities with their hosts of followers; until at last the whole gathering be-came absorbed into an orb of light which seemed to speed away to the East. And other phenomena were seen by some of us, each according to his ability.

Despite all the exhortation their Master had given them

The Life of Milarepa

miraculously thus, many were very depressed at the thought of having no relics. Once again the voice of our Master was heard, although this time there was no visual representation of him accompanying it. It said: 'Do not be so upset. For a solid relic go to the Amolika Boulder and you will find four letters miraculously carved thereon. Look at them with reverence and faith. Go and look beneath the boulder.'

Immediately we were off and searching and found them on the boulder where the cremation had been performed. Now those who needed it most had a relic stone to satisfy their hearts and it was established in the Lapchi-Chubar Monastery. The more advanced of the disciples, on the other hand, were quite comforted at their loss by the thought that wherever their Master had gone and obtained Buddhahood, they would in due course meet him again there. They also felt that Milarepa's life and example had instilled a new spirit into religions and into the minds of all men who heard of him. They knew, too, that the Initiations each had received, to be perfected by each one of them for himself, would be of service to himself and to others.

Then we remembered Milarepa's last Will and Testament in which he told us to dig up all the gold he had accumulated in his lifetime. With much curiosity we set about the task, for we were astonished at the thought that he could have made any money whatever, after the sort of life he had lived.

We turned up the hearth, therefore, as directed and found first a cotton square which our Master had worn. Wrapped in this was a knife, the handle being shaped into an awl and the back of the blade being a steel for kindling a fire. The blade was still good and sharp. With the knife was a lump of brown sugar and a bit of paper on which was written: 'The cloth and sugar, if cut with this knife will never be finished.

Cut as many strips as you can both from cloth and sugar and distribute them as widely as possible. All who taste the sugar or touch the cloth will derive spiritual benefit therefrom. These are the food and clothing of Milarepa when he united in trance with the Absolute and they have been blest by all the Buddhas. Even hearing the name of Milarepa will bring its own small reward to those who heed it. Whoever says that Milarepa possessed hidden gold let him be made to eat his words.'

This last amused us, despite our grief. Then at the bottom of the message was a short poem explaining more clearly the full significance of the food and cloth taken and worn by one who was in *Samadhi*, and adding that for one like himself, who had realised the Infinite, the whole Universe was as gold. What need was there then of man-valued metal? 'Do as I have commanded you, my sons and pupils,' he ended by writing.

And so we cut up the cloth and the sugar and distributed it freely and none was there who did not derive spiritual benefit therefrom. Evil dispositions and diseases fell away and were replaced by Faith and wholeness.

On every anniversary day of his departure, thereafter, flowers fell from the skies in beautiful colours and lay ankle-deep on the ground, then faded away again into air. Rainbows lit the skies and disappeared as the ceremonies were completed, and melodies filled the air also while the rites were in progress.

The Great Master left behind him his disciples to testify to the truth of this tale of his life which I have now finished. Many were these disciples and countless numbers of them achieved the supreme Aim and reached to Buddhahood. Many there were who entered upon the Path to Enlightenment as the result of his example and Teaching.

# Appendix

It may interest the reader to know what happened to some of us disciples in the years to come. The majority of those followers, men and women alike, who had been present at the death and funeral of the Guru, retired from life to live alone and meditate in solitude. I set out to take those articles which Milarepa had bequeathed on his deathbed to Dvagpo-Rimpoche who was then in another province. To him I gave the hat of Maitri and the staff and told him the whole story, at which he fainted away. On coming round he made many prayers to his late Guru and these are recorded in his own history of Milarepa's life, for he, too, wrote one. He afterwards invited me to stay with him and I gave him the Truths for Oral Transmission and then left and went to live in the Loro-Dol Monastery, to meditate for the rest of my life. The most advanced of the disciples did not die in the ordinary manner but were translated to the Realm of the Spirit and left no bodies behind them [Rechung, himself, was one of these], while the rest died in the normal way and left their bodies as relics for other less developed beings.

And so the great power of Milarepa, gained hardly and through much pain and suffering and self-discipline, suffused itself throughout the Universe and to other worlds beyond this one. Thus ends the history of the Great Yogi, Milarepa, who lived and died for the benefit of all sentient beings and obtained Buddhahood at the end.

Also published by Llanerch:

Rab'ia the Mystic,
Margaret Smith.

Flowers of a Mystic Garden,
Jan Ruysbroeck.

Symbolism of the Celtic Cross,
Derek Bryce.

Tao-te-ching
*(Lao-tsu)*

Wisdom of the Daoist Masters.
*(Lao Zi, Leh Zi, Zhuang Zi).*

For a complete list, write to Llanerch Publishers,
Felinfach, Lampeter, Dyfed, Wales, SA48 8PJ.